THE TAO OF
LEGAL WRITING

THE TAO OF
LEGAL WRITING

JUDITH M. STINSON

CAROLINA ACADEMIC PRESS
Durham, North Carolina

Library of Congress Cataloging-in-Publication Data

Stinson, Judith M.
  The Tao of legal writing / Judith M. Stinson.
    p. cm.
  Includes bibliographical references and index.
  ISBN 978-1-59460-633-5 (alk. paper)
  1. Legal composition. I. Title.

  KF250.S85 2009
  808'.06634—dc22   2009022324

Carolina Academic Press
700 Kent Street
Durham, NC 27701
Telephone (919) 489-7486
Fax (919) 493-5668
www.cap-press.com
www.caplaw.com

Printed in the United States of America

To Carlos and Mario

CONTENTS

ACKNOWLEDGMENTS

This book would not exist without substantial support, encouragement, and advice from a number of sources. First, I'd like to thank the Sandra Day O'Connor College of Law at Arizona State University for their generous support. I'd also like to thank Carissa and Andy Hessick for getting me back on track, Terry Pollman and Sam Moppett for countless hours of encouragement, and the writing faculty at ASU for all their help and years of teaching ideas. The national legal writing community has provided inspiration through conferences, articles, books, and conversations over the years, and I would especially like to thank attendees at the Ninth Annual Rocky Mountain Legal Writing Conference for their input, including Beth Cohen, Tonya Kowalski, Lance Long, Richard Neumann, and Suzanne Rabe.

I would like to thank the research assistants who helped with this book: Susan Anderson, Leta Hollon, and Stephanie Steele, and the law librarians who provided dedicated assistance: Amy Levine and Beth DiFelice.

A number of friends and colleagues reviewed drafts and provided helpful suggestions, and for that I am very grateful. I'd like to thank Sue Chesler, Stacey Dowdell, Tamara Herrera, Andy Hessick, Carissa Hessick, Marnie Hodahkwen, Jay Johnson, Amy Langenfeld,

Sam Moppett, Chad Noreuil, Cathy O'Grady, Terry Pollman, Zig Popko, Carrie Sperling, Connie Strittmatter, Doug Sylvester, and Tory Trotta.

Last but not least, I'd like to thank my parents – my dad for all his help with this particular project and his insights into the *Tao*, and both my mom and dad for making me believe I could do anything I wanted to do.

INTRODUCTION

After teaching legal writing – especially advanced legal writing – to students over the past fifteen years, I discovered that many of the concepts most central to effective legal writing do not lend themselves easily to explanation. But a parallel to those aspects of legal writing that are most difficult to articulate can be found in the *Tao Te Ching* and, to a lesser extent, eastern philosophies in general.

You need no prior exposure to the *Tao* to understand this book or the methods it describes, but for those interested, there are numerous sources that translate and provide commentary on this ancient Chinese philosophy. The *Tao*'s author, Lao-Tzu, was born about 570 B.C., and very little is known about him other than the book he authored. This legal writing book uses the translation by Stephen Mitchell;[1] each chapter begins and ends with a quote from a passage of the *Tao* that embodies the principle being discussed. Citations are to the relevant chapter in the *Tao*.

The word *Tao* translates into "*the way.*" Mitchell sums up the main concept embodied in the *Tao*, *wei wu wei* (literally "doing not-doing"), well:

---

1. Stephen Mitchell, *Tao Te Ching: A New English Version* (Perennial Classics 2000).

A good athlete can enter a state of body-awareness in which the right stroke or the right movement happens by itself, effortlessly, without any interference of the conscious will. This is a paradigm for non-action: the purest and most effective form of action. The game plays the game; the poem writes the poem; we can't tell the dancer from the dance.[2]

This book is about *the way* to write – like the *Tao* is about *the way* to live. The *Tao*'s basic point is simply this: don't force it; don't go against the nature of things. Learn that nature, accept it, and work within it – and you will be more successful. In legal writing, this requires six things:

- Be Flexible
- Don't Rush
- Break It Down
- Know When to Stop
- Reflect
- Let Go

The following chapters will explore each of these principles.

This book is designed for anyone who wants to be a better legal researcher and legal writer. Whether you are a law student, a paralegal, a lawyer, a judge, or anyone else who has had some training or experience in legal research and writing,[3] this book will provide a number of tools to help you become more proficient at legal analysis, legal research, and legal writing.

The first step in "advanced" legal research and writing is to refresh the skills learned in the introductory legal research and writing course: basic legal analysis, basic legal research, and basic objective and persuasive writing. This book will provide that refresher,

---

2. *Id.* at viii.

3. For those who completed a basic course many years ago, your practice experience in the meantime should provide all the background needed for you to jump into this book. For those with no prior legal writing experience, this book may still be helpful as a supplement to a basic legal research and writing text.

in a condensed format, as well as discuss matters that may make more sense now that you have had some exposure to and a little practice with the basic steps. Those additional matters include, for example, drafting a variety of documents including office memos, client letters, motions, appellate briefs, and even time sheets; researching regulations; finding an effective balance between book and computer research; and editing your own and others' work.

Many examples and discussions in this text are framed within the litigation setting because that is the model used most often in law schools, but the same principles apply to transactional drafting, with a few caveats. If you are interested specifically in drafting, especially a specialty area of drafting, you should also review a text or texts designed for that purpose.

This book is short for a reason: less is more. This text could go on for a thousand pages discussing various elements of legal analysis, legal research, and legal writing. My goal with this book is to provide the most effective techniques and tools for you to follow, and to provide them as quickly as possible. In a hundred pages or so, by reading this material and spending time thinking about these topics, you are likely to become better at legal analysis, legal research, and legal writing. Some of the information in this book will be familiar, and some will undoubtedly be new. Even with the familiar information, reading and thinking about it again is bound to be at least somewhat helpful.

Researching and writing are lifelong learning experiences – the more we practice these skills, the better we become. The more opportunities you have to research and write, and the more you try to incorporate the principles discussed in this text, the faster you will improve. In addition, thinking about legal research and writing in a new or slightly different way will add to the available choices about how to approach a problem or task. There are, and will be, moments of frustration with almost any project. But as you become more proficient in legal research and writing skills, you will feel less burdened by research and writing projects. Furthermore, as your skills improve, the more confidence you – and others – have in your analysis and in your communication of that analysis.

Mitchell paints the picture of the Tao's "central figure": the person "whose life is in perfect harmony with the way things are."[4] It is my genuine hope that after reading this book, legal writing becomes closer to a harmonious experience for you.

---

4. Mitchell, *supra* n. 1, at viii.

THE TAO OF
LEGAL WRITING

CHAPTER 1: THE WAY

True mastery can be gained
by letting things go their own way. – ch. 48

The *Tao* embodies principles of a natural flow and non-resistance. Incorporating these principles into your legal research and writing practices can help you become a more efficient and more effective legal writer. Your goal is to become what the *Tao* calls a "Master":

> *The ancient Masters were profound and subtle.*
> *Their wisdom was unfathomable.*
> *There is no way to describe it;*
> *all we can describe is their appearance.*
>
> *They were careful*
> *as someone crossing an iced-over stream.*
> *Alert as a warrior in enemy territory.*
> *Courteous as a guest.*
> *Fluid as melting ice.*
> *Shapable as a block of wood.*
> *Receptive as a valley.*
> *Clear as a glass of water.*
>
> *Do you have the patience to wait*
> *till your mud settles and the water is clear? – ch. 15*

Legal writing can be difficult to master, especially without ample opportunity to practice and receive individualized guidance. But this is no different than most skills that we master throughout our lives. Consider the skill of driving a car. Think about the steps a new driver has to consciously consider: put the key in the ignition. Turn the key to start the car. Make sure your foot is on the brake. The brake is the wide one in the middle (or on the left if the car is an automatic). Look in the mirrors. Put your hands on the steering wheel – 10 and 2.[1] Slowly – ever so slowly – lift your foot off the brake and apply it – again ever so slowly – to the gas. The gas pedal is the skinny one on the right. Be sure to signal. Signal up for right, down for left. And so on, and so on.

---

1. For those who did not learn by this method, this means to put your hands in the equivalent position that 10:00 and 2:00 occupy on a typical clock.

Just as we thought when we began driving, it seems like we should be able to – somehow innately – write legal documents effectively and efficiently. After all, we've been writing for years, just as we walked and rode bikes before we began driving. But as with driving, legal writing takes time to master. At first, we have to consciously think about every step.

For most of us, our early driving experiences resembled something like this: we took a class, took a test, and started practicing with a permit or an actual license. Not surprisingly, few of us were actually "good" as novices. But we had to learn somehow.

Chances are your legal writing experiences have taken a somewhat similar path. Take a class, take some tests (probably in the form of writing actual documents), and go practice your skill in the "real world."[2] But just like with driving, it takes a while to become truly proficient at legal writing.

The good news is that with driving, you probably did become proficient. Without even noticing it, you suddenly could drive without having to think about every step. You could accurately estimate the speed of oncoming traffic. You knew exactly how hard, or soft, to brake. And at some point, you could even drive well under difficult circumstances, such as during a blinding rainstorm.

Even if you are not yet an efficient and effective legal writer, you can become one. You have to start by reminding yourself of the steps – and working through them consciously. But at some point, most likely when you least expect it, you will be able to write without the constant struggle that most new legal writers face every time. And eventually, you will be able to masterfully draft even the most difficult documents under the most difficult circumstances. But that requires some patience on your part, and it requires you to surrender to forces beyond your control:

> *The Master sees things as they are,*
> *without trying to control them.*

---

2. The "real world" can mean a legal job or even law school – anywhere your written product is judged.

> *She lets them go their own way,*
> *and resides at the center of the circle. – ch. 29*

The need to control is, for many of us, strong; the law attracts Type A personalities who want things to go a certain way – our way. We can, in fact, influence outcomes:

> *The Master allows things to happen.*
> *She shapes events as they come. – ch. 45*

But that happens most when we work within the existing framework, rather than trying to overthrow the universe. Put bluntly:

> *Stop trying to control. – ch. 57*

Legal writing, like any other skill, is something that cannot be forced. Once you realize that writing (like other skills) becomes almost second nature after practice, you have taken an important first step on the path.

The Tao nourishes by not forcing. – ch. 81

CHAPTER 2: BE FLEXIBLE

Nothing in the world
is as soft and yielding as water.
Yet for dissolving the hard and inflexible,
nothing can surpass it.
The soft overcomes the hard;
the gentle overcomes the rigid.
Everyone knows this is true,
but few can put it into practice. – ch. 78

The practice of legal research and writing is evolving. Legal research tools and formats change over time; the dramatic increase in the availability and affordability of electronic legal research is just one example. In addition, readers' expectations change over time, as court rules change and accepted conventions expand.[1] And although the elements of legal analysis have not changed, the relevant materials and forums have changed over time as we move from a more case-based legal system to a more rule-based system. This shift requires that attorneys and law students learn to rely on statutes and administrative rules and to practice in tribunals other than traditional courts. To be a good legal researcher and writer, you need to have both a plan and some flexibility. As the expectations change, so should your approach and your ultimate work product.

Most specifically, flexibility in legal writing terms can be summed up as follows: respond to readers' expectations. Readers expect certain things, like letters to be single-spaced, memoranda to be organized a particular way, motions to be persuasive with your strongest argument first, and citations that include certain helpful information. Failing to meet these expectations is likely to negatively affect the reader's impressions of your document.

You therefore need to be conscious of what the reader expects of all documents, and what the reader expects of particular documents.[2] And beware; not all readers expect the same things. One of the biggest frustrations for legal writers is submitting a document to Lawyer A, who says to make change X; after making change X, Lawyer B says change X is wrong, and the document should be more like what you had in your first draft. Simply know that this occurs,

---

1. In contrast to legal research, legal writing conventions have remained more stable over time. Changes do occur, however, and the legal writer needs to be able to adapt to those changes. The most significant change is the marked increase in legal writing directed to arbitrators, mediators, or administrative law judges, some of whom are not legally trained. In addition, changes in conventions such as citation and the use of footnotes are occurring on a regular basis.

2. As you write, you also need to be aware of what language the reader expects you to use; this consideration is discussed in Chapter 4.

and that you are not the only writer to be caught in the middle between partners who do not see eye to eye.

To determine your reader's expectations, begin by thinking about your *audience*. Who is your audience? Is it a judge? If so, which judge (if you know)? Is it a partner? Which one? The parties? The client? Your opposing counsel? A law professor? What do you know about your audience? This information can often help you determine the expectations of your particular reader, rather than relying simply on the "common" reader.

A. What do legal readers expect of *all* documents?

Legal readers are busy. That means your task is to make the job of reading easier for them. First and foremost, documents should not be longer than absolutely necessary. Repetition, beyond what particular structural frameworks inherently include, is not favored. Second, documents should be easy to read,[3] free of errors, and generally "reader-friendly" – meaning you should use visual clues to help the reader understand your points easily. Here are a few quick suggestions on visual clues.

First, bold main headings. Note how this book's main sub-headings are bolded; that helps them stand out to a reader. More importantly, a reader trying to quickly understand the gist of your document can simply read through the bolded headings and know what your main arguments will be. Be sure that separate sections within a document (such as the "Argument" and "Conclusion" sections) stand out, generally by bolding them.

Second, number or letter sub-sections (and indent them further than the main headings). For example, within this chapter, the next section begins with a "B" at the left margin, and then the fist sub-section within that section is identified with a "1," and that heading is indented one tab from the section heading. Note that the entire text is not indented, just the heading. Next, the sub-sub sections are

---

3. Writing style is significant. That topic is discussed in Chapter 4, Part 4.

identified with an "a" and "b," and tabbed twice from the main heading (one from the sub-heading).[4]

Finally, generally avoid all caps and other conventions that may stand out (negatively) to the reader. Although document and section headings are often in all caps, sentences written in all capital letters are both hard to read and may suggest, in our e-mail culture, that you are yelling. In addition, spell check does not check words written in all capitals. Also avoid excessive use of bold or italicized text.

B. What do legal readers expect of *particular* documents?

Different documents have acquired different expected formats. Formats will, of course, vary somewhat from jurisdiction to jurisdiction and from reader to reader. As you begin each project, review any relevant court rules, office practice, a class syllabus, or other material to help you determine what your particular audience expects. Ask around and get informal feedback. And always, always look for samples – from a paralegal who has worked with the same partner, from others who have had experience with the same judge, or from professors. Reviewing good examples of what your audience expects can create a tremendous advantage.

The formats included here are common formats; if your office expects a different structure, by all means, follow your office's practice. But in the absence of guidance, the structures below should be a safe option.

1. Office Memoranda

a. Content

You have no doubt been told that a legal memorandum is an objective evaluation and application of the law to the facts, a docu-

---

4. Do not, however, label a heading "A" (or "1") if you have no "B" (or "2") – simply leave the heading, whether a main heading or sub-heading, on its own without a number or letter.

ment whose purpose is to inform the reader rather than advocate a particular position. That is true in law school, where your task is generally to identify which party is *likely* to prevail. In that memo, you should generally raise, objectively and openly, all strengths and weaknesses in your case.

But in practice – especially in big firms – office memos tend to be less objective. In much of law practice, memos are written less to decide whether, in theory, you should win or lose, and more to determine the best arguments for success (while at the same time acknowledging the inherent weaknesses). This does not mean you should fail to advise the partner that the case is almost certain to fail, especially when concrete precedent allows no other option. What it does mean is that you should, in addition to highlighting the strengths and weaknesses of the case, *argue* for your client. Clients want the best arguments, and are often willing to pay to fight it out. And even if the client is not paying, as with appointed counsel in criminal cases, objectivity may not be that important; your client may not receive a plea offer, so your goal may be to simply figure out the best defense strategy and how to poke holes in the government's case.

Hence, the label "objective" is really a misnomer; even in law school, as a writer your task is to justify what you think is the most likely outcome. In sum, then, you are really attempting to *persuade* the reader that your analysis is correct.

b. Structure

Formats for office memoranda vary quite a bit. As noted above, follow the structure that your particular reader wants, even if it is not the structure with which you are most familiar.

The most common formats are listed here:

> I.   Issue(s)
> II. Brief Answer(s)
> III. Facts
> IV. Discussion
> V.   Conclusion

I.   Factual Background
II. Question(s) Presented
III. Brief Answer(s)
IV. Discussion
V.   Conclusion

I.   Introduction
II. Issue(s)
III. Conclusion
IV. Discussion

Regardless of which overall structure you adopt, the purpose and content of each section within that structure is generally consistent.

i. Issue (or Question Presented)

First, add an "s" to the heading ("issues" or "questions presented") if you have more than one issue. When you have more than one, number them for the reader. Second, issues should generally be limited to one sentence and be case specific. The "under / does / when" format is especially helpful: under ____ (the applicable law), does _____ (the legal result) occur when _____ (the relevant facts)? Generally, framing the issue as a question makes it easier for the reader. In the United States Supreme Court, note the convention varies; questions presented begin with "Whether" and then include the same information above. Although this creates an incomplete sentence, it is the format accepted – and more importantly expected – in that Court. I would avoid using it, though, in usual office memoranda.

ii. Brief Answer (or Answer)

As with the issue, add an "s" ("brief answers") if you have more than one issue/answer. The brief answer should briefly explain or summarize your answer to the issue presented, and if you have more than one issue, the brief answers should directly correspond to (and match, in terms of numbering) those issues. Citations to authority are generally unnecessary in the brief answer. Furthermore, the answer needs to be both direct and short; generally, one paragraph is sufficient. Finally, use "buzz words" – the terms of art that define the applicable legal standard – to begin to acquaint your reader with the law as well as how it applies to your particular facts.

iii. Facts (or Factual Background)

In theory, the facts section should be the easiest to write. Be sure, though, to include all facts you use elsewhere, and to include only those facts relevant to the outcome.

iv. Discussion

This section is the meat of the document. Chapter 4 addresses the analytical and organizational skills needed to draft an effective discussion section. Briefly, the discussion section is generally organized internally in the following order: conclusion, rule, rule proof or explanation (a discussion of the governing authorities), application/analysis (where you directly apply your facts to the law you identified as relevant), and conclusion.

v. Conclusion

The conclusion section is probably the one that varies most; some readers prefer incredibly short conclusions (often only one sentence), but others expect a longer, more thorough conclusion that highlights the main points of analysis and includes a recommendation for future action.

vi. Introduction

If you follow the format that begins with an introduction, that section generally contains a brief overview of the issues and likely outcomes, along with the relevant facts. Note that memoranda following this format sometimes omit the brief answer section (and sometimes even the issues, as they are covered in the introduction).

2. Client Letters

a. Content

Client letters are less objective than office memoranda, but still not (usually) fully persuasive. A client letter should inform the client about the strengths and weaknesses of her case. You generally want the client to feel you are on her "side," though, and it is easier to do that if you are positive about the case. That being said, client letters can serve to protect you from legal malpractice liability later, so you should not omit damning information or analysis solely to please the client. In the end, most clients prefer to know they are likely to lose (and have the option of settling) rather than to lose after a prolonged and expensive battle. Getting the right tone can be tricky with client letters; keep the client's perspective in mind, tailor your writing to your particular client, and aim for a letter that is easy to read yet informative.

b. Structure

The structure of the typical client letter is very similar to that of a memo, although usually less formal and often without explicit divisions between the sections. Traditional paragraph divisions generally suffice. As with a memo, client letters usually follow this basic format:

> I.   Introduction
> II. Facts
> III. Discussion
> IV. Conclusion

The introduction usually recites the issue you have been asked to address on behalf of the client. The facts summarize the facts relied upon in reaching your conclusion, and that section should make it explicit to the reader that your analysis is based on those facts; hence, if there are any inaccuracies or omissions, the client should advise you so you can modify your analysis. The discussion is essentially the same as a discussion in an office memorandum (described briefly in section B(1)(b)(iv), and more thoroughly in Chapter 4). Unless your client is especially sophisticated, you should probably avoid using excessive legal jargon. Finally, the letter should include your ultimate conclusion. As noted earlier, client letters are generally single-spaced.

3. Complaints

a. Content

Because a complaint initiates a particular lawsuit, the most significant factor affecting the content of your complaint is the underlying substantive law involved in your claim. Complaints generally must include three components: a statement of jurisdiction, a claim for relief, and a demand for judgment.[5] Aside from that, how much detail to include (or not) is usually up to the writer. With regard to what to include, if you are starting with a form, be sure to research your own case both factually and legally. You need to include enough facts to make your case (and survive a 12(b)(6) motion to dismiss), and you need to be sure the law is accurate. Many form books are generic; not all state laws are the same, and even if the form book you are using is state-specific, it could be wrong.

b. Structure

Structurally, you have a lot of options. Complaints are generally formatted with numbered paragraphs, and different writers prefer varying levels of detail and information in each paragraph. As with all documents, follow your office's practice or own preference, but be sure to check court rules on the requirements for that particular court. Be especially mindful of the local rules; the soft-cover handbook with all of the court rules that apply in your jurisdiction – federal district and appellate, state trial and appellate, city courts, traffic courts, etc. – is immensely helpful for this purpose.

---

5. Rule 8(a) of the Federal Rules of Civil Procedure requires these three components, and most complaints, even in state court, include the same information.

4. Demand Letters

a. Content

Unlike client letters (and office memoranda), demand letters are expressly persuasive – that is, all parties expect you to try and persuade the reader of the outcome you prefer, not to objectively analyze the strengths and weaknesses of your client's case. You are now seeking a result – trying to convince your opponent to take some action (or stop acting). What exactly are you seeking? How can you get that result? In addition, your audience is also different; you now are writing to an external decision-maker.[6]

In general terms, we persuade in three ways, in this order of importance:

- substance
- organization
- style/word choice

Substantively, be sure you have logical, sound arguments. Organization is discussed below. Style and word choice are discussed more fully in Chapter 4, but briefly, your language shifts from that used in an office memorandum. Rather than conceding weaknesses, you task now is to bury them. Similarly, use more detail for points you want to emphasize and want the reader to remember; use less detail for points you want to downplay and want the reader to forget.

b. Structure

Structurally, a demand letter follows the same basic pattern as a client letter: an introduction (which often includes the most basic facts), the argument (which parallels the discussion, but is now persuasively framed), and a conclusion (which asks, in specific terms, for what you want and when).

---

6. In addition, a demand letter is sometimes required by law prior to initiating a lawsuit. In those instances, be sure to include all information necessary for that particular claim.

5. Motions

a. Content

Like demand letters, motions are expressly persuasive. Because they are filed with a court, however, motions are generally more formal and detailed. Your goal with any motion is to get the court to grant some request, and you therefore need to convince the court that granting your request is proper. You can file a motion for just about anything: to continue, to suppress evidence, to compel disclosure, to amend. For anything you want or need the judge's permission to do, you can file a motion.[7]

b. Structure

A formal motion page is generally required, but the meat of the document is the Memorandum of Law in Support of the Motion. The Memorandum generally includes an introduction, an argument, and a conclusion. Within the argument section, it is important that you begin with your strongest point; some readers will not continue if it is weak. Hence, the order is as follows: make your strongest point first, put your weakest point in the middle, and include another strong point at the end. Follow this basic format for the overall document, as well as within each section, within each paragraph, and within each sentence.[8]

Motions are governed by court rules. Be sure to check the applicable rules (including local rules) before drafting a motion. Specific motions, such as a Motion for Summary Judgment, often need a separate Statement of Material Facts (a generic introduction is not enough).

---

7. The best motion, though, is one that you never had to write. If, with a phone call, you can get your opponent to agree to something that the judge doesn't have to approve, do it! And even if the judge has to approve it, if the other side agrees, the motion can generally be shorter (unless you expect the judge to object on her own, in which case, you need to persuade her why she should grant the motion).

8. Of course, you won't always have three issues. Don't feel the need to invent issues or arguments solely to follow this persuasive structure.

Absent a governing court rule, the basic format for most motions is as follows:

> I. Introduction
> II. Argument
> III. Conclusion

The introduction explains to the judge what you are seeking, in basic terms, along with the court rule that gives the court the authority to grant your request. It also summarizes the relevant facts. The argument is the guts of your motion, and it follows the same structure as that used in a memorandum's discussion section. That structure is discussed in detail in Chapter 4. The conclusion is generally very short – a sentence is common – and it asks the court to grant your request (naming that request specifically).

6. Appellate Briefs

a. Content

An appellate brief is the most formal document most lawyers ever write, so it is not taught as part of the mandatory legal writing program in many law schools. Although more formal, an appellate brief is not all that different from a motion; you are making an argument (or a series of arguments) to an impartial decision-maker, and you are seeking a particular result. Hence, it is beneficial to start by thinking of an appellate brief as more like a motion than unlike one.

There are key differences, though. Because they are filed after the trial court has resolved the matter initially, appellate briefs almost always contain a discussion of the relevant standard of review, whether as a separate section or within the argument. They also contain several unique document sections. The Summary of the Argument section, for example, is incredibly significant; this should be the last section you draft, and it needs to be both persuasive and concise. If you plan to draft appellate briefs in practice or for moot court, I would strongly suggest buying a good text on appellate advocacy.[9]

b. Structure

As with some motions, appellate briefs are subject to a host of court rules. The rules for the United States Supreme Court, for example, are incredibly detailed. To highlight a few of the technical rules, briefs must be filed in booklet format, on 6⅛ × 9¼ inch pages, with a specific typeface and size, margins, and type of paper ("opaque, unglazed, and not less than 60 pounds in weight").[10] All courts have requirements on the page limits, the paper size, the number of copies to file, and other details, including what sections are required. A brief to the United States Supreme Court, for example, should have all of the following sections:[11]

I.	Cover Page
II.	Questions Presented
III.	Parties to the Proceeding
IV.	Table of Contents
V.	Table of Authorities
VI.	Opinions Below
VII.	Statement of Jurisdiction
VIII.	Relevant Enacted Law
IX.	Statement of the Case
X.	Summary of the Argument
XI.	Argument
XII.	Conclusion

The Table of Contents helps the reader see a snapshot of your argument, both structurally and persuasively. Take the time to present

---

9. Mary Beth Beazley's *A Practical Guide to Appellate Advocacy* (2d ed., Aspen 2006) is an excellent source.

10. S. Ct. R. 33(1)(a), (b), and (c).

11. *Id.* at 34.1; 24.1(a); 24.1(b); 24.1(c); 24.1(d); 24.1(e); 24.1(f); 24.1(g); 24.1(h); 24.1(i); 24.1(j); *see also* Beazley, *supra* n.9, at 123–31.

it clearly and effectively, much like an outline. Within the Argument, follow the structure discussed in Chapter 4, being sure to use persuasive headings – also called "point headings" – to enable your reader to quickly and effectively understand your argument in summary form and to quickly identify the various arguments within the larger brief.[12]

7. Time Sheets/Bills

Although few law students think about the need for effective writing when it comes to time sheets, managing partners at law firms think about this topic regularly. Time sheets serve both an informative and a persuasive function – you need to persuade the client that your time was spent effectively and that the client should pay. Each office has its own expected content and structure, but in a basic sense, you are more likely to be effective with your time sheets if you use active voice, start each entry with a verb, and show the *results* of your work (the document produced, etc.) in the entry.

C. Final Thoughts

We all have ideas of what a particular document could or should contain and how it could or should be structured. Those ideas are helpful, and should inform your final decisions. As a legal writer, though, keep in mind that your task is to be flexible enough to meet the needs and expectations of your audience and to accomplish your purpose. The trick is to bend without breaking.

> *The hard and stiff will be broken.*
> *The soft and supple will prevail. – ch. 76*

---

12. One prominent jurist mentioned a brief filed in court that listed the various arguments only by number – and there were 26 of them. Hence, the first argument, rather than being identified with a one-sentence summary of the point, was simply called "Argument 1," and so on. This format was not helpful to the Court when trying to locate a particular argument.

CHAPTER 3: DON'T RUSH

Rushing into action, you fail.
Trying to grasp things, you lose them.
Forcing a project to completion,
you ruin what was almost ripe. – ch. 64

Legal writing takes time. We would all prefer to finish sooner, but the reality is that most things, including legal writing, just can't be rushed. Hence, your task is to plan ahead and allow ample time for the process. That means allowing more time than you might expect for each project, and allowing more time than you might expect to internalize the principles in this book.

A. How Can I Avoid the Impulse to Rush?

First, plan realistically. I have yet to meet a person who routinely finishes writing projects in less time than he or she expected. You will be far more likely to succeed if you expect the writing to take two to three times longer than you would originally estimate. Imagine you are assigned to draft a memorandum; after your initial review of the file and some very basic research, you think you can conduct all the necessary research and draft a suitable memo in ten hours. Stop and adjust your thinking here: instead of ten hours, plan on spending twenty to thirty. If in fact you overestimate the actual time it will take, you finish early. Celebrate.

Second, budget your time accordingly, moving between various stages in the writing process (these stages will be discussed in Chapter 4). Thinking, researching, outlining, writing, and revising are not steps in a linear process, but part of a circular process that moves between the various parts. Allot enough time for each part of the process, knowing that you are likely to circle through the various stages. Most significantly, allow yourself enough time for research so you don't feel you have to begin writing too soon. By the same token, don't spend seventy-five percent of your total time on research, leaving yourself only a few hours to actually write. The inevitable end-product will suffer under such a scenario. Yet many legal writers, uncomfortable with putting pen to paper (or, more appropriately, fingers to keyboard), procrastinate by researching a project to death in an effort to avoid actually writing. Avoid this temptation. Realistically budget your time for each task at the beginning, and try to stick to it.

Third, start projects early. Rather than waiting until the day before a project is due – even if you realistically think that project will take only five hours – review it and conduct some preliminary research the day (or week) you get the project. By starting a project early, your thinking has more time to gel; you will end up with a better product simply by virtue of allowing your ideas to crystallize over time. Some of the most important analytical discoveries hit us at odd times – in the shower, on our drive in to work, or at the ballgame. These moments don't really add to the number of days or weeks we allotted for a project; we have to shower and drive to work anyway.[1] Allowing your mind to wander and think about how to best approach a problem, the answer often appears, as if by magic. Rushing though a project almost guarantees that these opportunities for inspiration will be forever lost.

The unfortunate realities of law practice are that we can never spend as long as we would like on each project. But we almost always end up spending more time than we budgeted – suggesting that if we just budget longer from the start, we will feel less pressured and less rushed in the end (while spending the same amount of time we would have anyway).

B. How Can I Be More Efficient, and Hence, Avoid the *Need* to Rush?

Here is the ironic rub: the more we rush, the less effective we are – and hence, the more we need to rush. Think about the last time you were in a hurry to get out of the house (so you wouldn't be late for work, to school, to meet friends, etc.). You likely rushed about the house, trying to grab everything you needed. Did you get out of the house any faster than when you calmly and rationally left home on any other day? Probably not. Or try to rush and put your socks on as fast as you can. Chances are you will have to try several

---

1. And if we are wise, we will make time for unwinding and for the truly important people and events in our lives.

times, catching your toes and otherwise causing yourself to take longer than if you just put each sock on at a normal pace. The reality is that we can't accomplish as much when we rush. Hence, the first trick to becoming more efficient so you don't have to rush is – simply – not to rush.

Second, practice will help. The more you write, the easier it becomes to write. Practice doesn't necessarily make perfect (although it makes it much more likely your writing skills will improve), but practice almost always increases your effectiveness. Recall the driving analogy: when you first learned to drive, every move required a conscious thought, and the thoughts came slowly. Which way do I push the lever to signal a right turn? Up, or down? After awhile, it became automatic, and, for those who still use a turn signal, you don't even need to think about which direction to push the lever. Reading this book and working on the skills discussed will help you become a more efficient writer. In the end, this will decrease your need to rush.

Third, discover your "zone." Although circumstances don't always allow us to work when and where we feel most efficient, you can often adjust tasks so you can spend the majority of your writing time when and where you can be most efficient. Whatever your "zone" is – meaning where or when you can write best – for example, in that favorite chair, in the deserted corner of the library, from 5 a.m. to 10 a.m., or on Saturdays when the phone rings less – become aware of when and where you write best. Then, try to schedule your time so you can write under those conditions. Take care of phone calls and other more routine tasks at off times/locations, and plan to do the hardest work when you are most capable.

Of course, you won't always have the luxury of waiting until you are in your zone to write, but if you are conscious about it, you can maximize your effectiveness by using that time wisely. Nothing is more frustrating than to spend hours at a movie and then come home to write, but discover you have writer's block; if you had written first (during your productive time) and gone to the movie afterward, you probably would have accomplished a great deal and still enjoyed the movie just as much.

Life is too short to rush – even life in the practice of law. And it's counterproductive. If you really want to finish a project, slow down. Rather than forcing it to completion, you are likely to discover that, in some sense, the project completed itself.

> *He who rushes ahead*
> *doesn't go far. – ch. 24*

CHAPTER 4: BREAK IT DOWN

Confront the difficult
while it is still easy;
accomplish the great task
by a series of small acts. – ch. 63

The gist of this chapter is that writers need to attack each project step-by-step. Many writers procrastinate in large part because the task seems too ominous to tackle; it seems impossible to write a coherent and effective forty-three-page brief, so the writer waits until the last minute, essentially guaranteeing that the final product will be incoherent and ineffective. You can be much more effective with each project when you approach the final product by considering a series of steps – and consciously work through them until the process becomes automatic. At that point, you can move to a more holistic approach, modifying the steps as needed based on the specific project and an overall sense of the document's effectiveness. This chapter will describe the legal writing process, discuss the tasks within the writing process, and get you to move from thinking to actually writing.

A. What Is the "Legal Writing Process"?

Legal writing is a process. It is not a linear task that we can march through from start to finish and then be "done." Rather, legal writing requires that we think and operate in a circular fashion, moving back and forth between issues, legal research, legal rules, and facts, often modifying our earlier positions and conclusions.[1] Few of us are the legal writing equivalent of Beethoven, composing the perfect legal analysis in our heads and simply writing it down for others to follow. For most of us, the writing process is how we learn – by attempting to communicate our analysis, we discover where we have confusion, what needs to be changed, etc. Even after we have mastered the issues, the law, and the facts, we need to return to the various components of our document to revise and polish, lest we fail to effectively communicate our legal analysis to our reader. In short, *the legal writing process includes repeatedly thinking, re-*

---

1. Be open to the possibility that your final conclusion may be quite different from your initial assessment. Furthermore, be open to the possibility of any or no solution; this will help you discover the *best* solution.

searching, outlining, writing, and revising, and moving freely between these five tasks; all are integral components of the process that results in the final written product.

Following this *process* of legal writing – that is, the steps necessary to develop an effective written product – will, in the end, result in consistently better written products. The goal is to have you – the writer – think and make conscious decisions about the steps necessary to analyze and write each project.

Furthermore, although it is imperative to consciously think about the *process* of legal writing to ultimately be an effective legal writer, considering the requirements of the final written *product* will make it more likely that you fulfill those requirements. The final written product can be judged in a number of ways, but most readers will consider, with varying degrees of relative importance, the following four main categories: 1) analysis; 2) structure; 3) style; and 4) format.

These stages, in progressively decreasing order of importance, should help you focus your time and attention appropriately. For example, if a document includes faulty legal analysis, the writing style is of little significance. Similarly, if the structure of a document fails to communicate the relationship between issues or sub-issues, the format of the document is inconsequential. This is not to say that the lower stages are unimportant; on the contrary, each stage is essential. But if a document has problems at a higher level, correcting (or even addressing) problems at a lower level is futile.

B. What Do I Need to Do During the Writing Process?

It is somewhat odd to include a linear list of numbered "writing process" tasks when the entire point of this chapter is that your writing process should not be linear. Rather, it should be circular and free flowing between the various stages. However, the only way to discuss each core component effectively is to do so somewhat isolated from the other core components – to "break it down." Just recall, as you read each section, that you must move between these tasks regularly and circularly to be a successful writer.

The five tasks you need to complete during this writing process are: 1) thinking; 2) researching; 3) outlining; 4) writing; and 5) revising.

BREAK IT DOWN, PART 1: THINK

A good traveler has no fixed plans
and is not intent upon arriving.
A good artist lets his intuition
lead him wherever it wants.
A good scientist has freed himself of concepts
and keeps his mind open to what is. – ch. 27

Like the *Tao*, in legal writing, the more open-minded you can be, the more successful you can be. Although we often form preliminary conclusions, and we are often asked to justify a particular conclusion, it is still helpful to approach the issue with an open mind so you can spot counter-arguments and potential weaknesses.[1] As a preliminary matter in this "thinking" stage, you need to determine your *purpose* for writing. What do you hope to accomplish with the ultimate written document? Are you seeking summary judgment? If so, are you seeking judgment on the entire case, or just part of it? Is dismissal unlikely, but is there some chance a court will rule in your client's favor such that your opponent might be persuaded to settle? Is the ultimate goal settlement, or to improve your chances at trial? Are you trying to create a record for appeal? Are you trying to get a good grade? If you cannot articulate what you hope to accomplish, it is highly unlikely that your final work product will be successful.

Whatever your purpose, determine it and be conscious of it as you move through each stage of the legal writing process. The most embarrassing moment for many new lawyers is when they are asked "what are you asking for?" and they have no clear answer.

Once you have determined your purpose, you are ready for the bulk of the "thinking" – *analysis*. Effective legal analysis is both the first and most important step to creating an effective written document. If its analysis is faulty, the most beautiful prose in the world cannot save the document.

If you have had some prior exposure to legal writing, it may come as no surprise to you that the way lawyers analyze a legal problem can be represented with the acronym "IRAC." You likely have had significant exposure to IRAC and substantial opportunity to work with that paradigm, but a refresher here, highlighting some important tips you may have forgotten or never been told, is warranted.

---

1. This is especially true for law school exams.

"IRAC" generally includes these four components: Issue, Rule, Application (also called Analysis), and Conclusion. This structure represents the logical organization for deductive reasoning, the essential analytical skill used by lawyers. Each component is discussed in more detail below.

I	=	Issue
R	=	Rule
A	=	Application/Analysis
C	=	Conclusion

1. Issue

On rare occasions, the issue is directly given to you. On those days, just know that your task may be more difficult tomorrow. Most of the time, you need to determine the issue, or at least a part of it, on your own.

How can you determine the issue in a legal problem? The "Issue" is a result of the combination of facts and legal rules. There are two types of Issues. First, *legal issues* occur when the legal rule itself is ambiguous; this type of issue involves determining the proper standard to apply.[2] Second, *factual issues* occur when the application of facts to a clear legal test is ambiguous; this type of issue involves determining whether particular facts meet a stated legal test.[3] Furthermore, many issues will have sub-issues, such as when two or more elements of a rule are in question, either legally or factually.

---

2. Not all disputes about the rule, though, create "issues." Some disputes – legal or factual – are irrelevant based on the surrounding circumstances. For example, assume the common law is unclear about whether a renter, as opposed to a property owner, may sue another for nuisance. If, under the facts of your client's case, the plaintiff is the property owner, this ambiguity in the legal test is irrelevant and does not create an "issue."

3. Note that a "factual issue" is different from an instance where you *do not know* the facts. In the latter instance, you should state what fact is missing, why it is relevant, and the potential outcomes depending on the ultimate fact.

When faced with a problem that presents more than one main issue, address the legal issue or issues first (the questions about what the law is for your particular case). Once the standard has been articulated, you are ready to resolve any factual issues.

Because issues involve a combination of facts and legal rules, you cannot determine the issues until you fully understand the facts. In addition, often some preliminary legal research is required before you can precisely determine the relevant legal issue(s).

The starting point for identifying issues is identifying each party's potential claims and the governing rules for each claim or defense. Focus on the points where a good faith argument can be made both *for* and *against* a particular conclusion.

Consider the following example:

> Assume a reasonable person could interpret Arizona's robbery statute to require the victim fear for his safety. Assume another reasonable person could interpret the same test to focus solely on the defendant's objective actions, leaving the victim's state of mind irrelevant. Here, you have identified a *"legal issue"*: what is the proper test?
>
> Next, assume that fear is required, and your facts indicate the victim told the defendant, "You must be kidding; I'm not giving you a dime." Yet, when responding to police questioning following the incident, the victim relayed he was "terrified" of the defendant. You have now identified a *"factual issue"*: did the victim "fear" for his safety sufficiently to meet this element of Arizona's robbery statute?

2. Rule

Rules take on a variety of forms. The "rule" may be stated in one place, as with a statute. The legislature may have neatly and clearly ordered the rule into separate, nicely numbered elements. Each element may be clear and unambiguous. On the other (more likely) hand, you may have to **synthesize** the "rule" from several sources.

For example, you may need to read three separate cases with vary-ing holdings to determine the complete rule that governs a partic-ular issue. To synthesize an overall rule in this situation, it is often helpful to draft a one-sentence rule for each case, and then read all the sentences to determine what they, as a group, mean. Then, you can draft a one sentence "synthesized" rule which represents the cur-rent state of law.[4]

In addition, even when a statute governs the situation, often the statute alone does not provide the complete rule. Statutes are in-tended to be prospective and broad, and courts, through their de-cisions, interpret the language of statutes in specific contexts. Con-sider the following example:

> Assume that in a criminal shoplifting case, a defendant has been charged with violating a particular state statute. That statute reads as follows: "It is illegal for a person to take prop-erty without paying from a place of business when the prop-erty is marked for sale." Although this appears to create a rel-atively neat, clean rule, assume that the state supreme court recently held that in order to violate this statute, the defen-dant "must intend to permanently deprive the business of the property." Now, rather than using only the statute as your rule, you must combine the statute and the case holding into one synthesized rule. That rule might look something like this:
>
> Shoplifting is illegal and occurs when all of the following el-ements are met:
> 1) a person takes property;
> 2) without paying;
> 3) from a place of business;
> 4) when the property is marked for sale; and
> 5) when the person intends to permanently deprive the business of the property.

---

4. Rules do not always need to be limited to one sentence, but in general, keep them as short as possible.

Note how the portion of the rule added by the court is included in the rule, rather than stating two separate rules about shoplifting. The reader needs to know immediately what the complete rule is; you can (and will) later describe how and where you found each portion of this rule. But it is your job, as the person conducting the legal analysis and communicating that analysis to others, to simplify this task for the reader and to state the rule as one synthesized test.

In addition, note how the "rule" above is divided into numbered *elements*. Legal analysis can be greatly simplified by breaking rules into their requisite elements. The test is now framed as a series of requirements; each must be met in order for the defendant to be convicted. If any one element is missing, acquittal is proper. Breaking a rule into its parts has several advantages. First, consistent with the theme of this chapter, any task is simplified by breaking it into its parts. Second, expressly breaking the rule up into elements will assure that you consider all relevant portions of the rule. Third, breaking the rule into elements will help later in the outlining and writing stages of the project. Most significantly, breaking the rule into elements will simplify and clarify the analysis for the reader, making it more likely your document will be effective.

Although most rules can and should be broken down into their elements, not all rules have elements. Some rules are based on *factors*. The distinction between elements and factors is somewhat subtle, but incredibly important. Elements are dispositive; that is, they form a list of items that must be met or must not be met to satisfy the legal test. Factors, on the other hand, are items that are relevant to determining whether the legal test is satisfied, but none is dispositive. Consider the following example:

> Assume the shoplifting test in your jurisdiction has been phrased like this: "in determining whether a person committed shoplifting, the court considers all relevant circumstances, such as where the incident occurred, where the person was apprehended, what was taken, whether there was any attempt to

> pay for the item, whether the person hid the property while in the store, whether the person bought any other items, whether the person had any money in his or her possession, and whether the person made any statements regarding the item or items taken." This is a "factors" test, rather than an "elements" test.

Under this kind of test, not all factors must be met, and not all factors even need to weigh in favor of conviction. All are taken into consideration in deciding whether to convict, though. Some factors may weigh more than others, and a court (or legislature) may expressly state which are most significant.

Some rules combine elements and factors, such as the test for determining whether a confession is admissible. Consider the following example:

> *Miranda v. Arizona* requires a criminal defendant be advised of various rights, including the right to remain silent, before his confession is admissible. The *Miranda* rule, however, only applies to confessions obtained during "custodial interrogation." Hence, the defendant must prove two *elements* to suppress a statement made without the requisite warnings: 1) he was in custody; and 2) his statement was the result of interrogation. However, in determining whether the defendant was "in custody" (one of the elements), the court looks to all the surrounding circumstances, which involves examining *factors*.

See *Miranda v. Arizona*.[5]

When stating rules that are based on elements, legislatures and courts often use phrases such as "the following circumstances are re-

---

5. 384 U.S. 436 (1966).

quired" or "these are necessary," and they sometimes use the explicit term "elements." When stating rules that are based on factors, legislatures and courts often use phrases such as "totality of the circumstances," "all relevant evidence," and "factors to consider include."

Sometimes, as noted above with regard to "issues," there is genuine dispute as to which of two or more conflicting rules applies. This occurs when, for example, there is a question about which jurisdiction's law will govern, there is a question about whether a state has adopted a restatement provision or retained the common law, or there is a question about the applicable standard of review. In those instances, do your best to predict which will govern – or if you are drafting a persuasive document, argue why the choice you prefer is correct – but if doubt still exists, state both conflicting rules and then proceed to analyze your facts under each rule separately.

In addition to problems concerning conflicting rules, you may be called upon to analyze a case of first impression, meaning a situation that has not yet been considered in your jurisdiction. When the rule has not yet been stated in any capacity, you must do your best to predict what the rule would be from other available rules. For example, does your jurisdiction generally follow the restatement? If so, can you argue they would follow the restatement rule in this context?

Regardless of the type of rule you are using, whether based on elements, factors, or both, or a case of first impression requiring you to create and argue for a new rule, it is important to clearly state the rule – the complete, synthesized rule – for each main issue. You will later break the rule down and separately consider any disputed sub-issues/elements.

There are several important considerations for the "rule" portion of your analysis:

a. Choice of Law

Address and decide this first. Regardless of which court is hearing the dispute, what is the applicable law? If in federal court only by virtue of diversity jurisdiction, state law will apply on the substantive issue. Consider, and research if necessary, which state's law governs. If in state court, but the party is raising a federal law claim, federal substantive law will apply.

b. Hierarchy of Authority

All rules are not created equally. First, only *binding* rules will require a particular outcome; rules that are merely persuasive may be helpful, but because courts are not required to follow them, they are generally less significant. Hence, rely on non-binding authority only when no binding authority resolves the issue.

Binding rules include constitutional and statutory provisions from the applicable jurisdiction. Holdings from published opinions by courts in the applicable jurisdiction are also binding when they are decided by the same court or a court at a higher level than the court which will hear your dispute.

In contrast, *persuasive* (also called "non-binding") authority includes primary authorities from other jurisdictions, including constitutions, statutes, and cases, as well as *all* secondary authorities. It also includes trial court decisions, and it includes appellate decisions if you are before the highest court in the jurisdiction or before a different appellate division in a non-unified court of appeals, such as the federal system. Finally, non-binding authority includes "dicta." Dicta are statements in a judicial opinion that are unnecessary to the resolution of the narrow issue before the court. Dictum (the singular form of dicta) often sounds remarkably good; for some reason, many courts express rules most clearly when those rules are not directly applicable to the dispute before the court. But statements of rules that are not necessary for resolving the case before the court – or of what a court *would* do *if* confronted with a particular circumstance – are not binding on future disputes. They are dicta only, and as such, they are always only persuasive. Often, however, dicta can be very persuasive, especially when from the highest court in a jurisdiction.

Second, within the category of binding authority (or persuasive authority if no binding authority exists), certain rules are paramount. Begin with any applicable constitutional provision. Next, look to statutes. Third, review any applicable administrative regulations[6] and consider case law.

c. Weight of Authority

Within each category of authority, some sources carry more weight than others. For example, within the non-binding category of secondary authority, a law review article written by Lawrence Tribe on the constitutionality of a particular law will carry more weight than a one-paragraph entry in *American Jurisprudence Second*.[7] Similarly, on-point statutes restrict case law, unless the statute is declared unconstitutional.

A few additional factors are relevant with case law: the level of the deciding court, the depth of analysis on your issue, the age of the decision, and the factual similarities or differences with your case. First, cases from the highest court will generally carry more weight than cases from lower courts. Second, the more a particular case discusses an issue, the greater, in general, its weight. Cases with a cursory discussion of an issue will generally carry less weight. Third, older decisions will, in general, carry less weight than more recent decisions. Finally, cases that are more factually similar to your case – or significantly different in a way that helps the analysis – will carry more weight than cases with few opportunities for factual comparisons and contrasts.

Throughout, the phrase "in general" is intended to demonstrate that weight of authority is affected by a number of factors, and the writer must consider all relevant components of each case to determine which, in the end, carries the *most* weight. Include less weighty cases later, perhaps with parenthetical explanations, or consider omitting them entirely if they do not add to the argument.[8]

---

6. For the most part, this chapter refers to statutes and cases as the main sources of rules. Administrative regulations have separate considerations that are discussed in Part 2 of this chapter.

7. That is not to say that *American Jurisprudence* is not a useful research tool. It means a court is less likely to be persuaded by an anonymous *American Jurisprudence* author than by a noted constitutional law scholar.

8. Of course, this assumes the reader is also complying with the "choice of law" and "hierarchy of authority" points above.

d. Framing the Rule

When thinking about (and eventually stating) your rule, use "buzz words" and terms of art. "Buzz words" and terms of art are those words and phrases that legislatures and courts use consistently (or at least somewhat consistently) to refer to specific tests or elements within those tests. Using those same terms will aid the reader by identifying the standard the legislature or court adopted and by providing consistency. Avoid varying your language or terminology when discussing these key concepts; although this may appear stylistically preferable, it will only confuse the reader. For example, in this chapter many key concepts are bolded or italicized, such as "elements" and "factors." These are, in effect, "buzz words."

Using the *Miranda* example, which requires a defendant be "in custody" to trigger various warnings, if the writer switches between "under arrest," "held by the police," and "in custody," the reader will wonder whether there is a legally-significant difference between these three phrases. Instead, be consistent and stick to the term or phrase used by the legislature or court. Furthermore, using quotation marks for buzz words or terms of art when first introduced helps the reader understand that this particular phrasing is legally significant.

e. Proving the Rule

When communicating your analysis, whether in written or oral form, you will need to prove that the rule you articulate is in fact the rule.[9] In the "thinking" stage, this requires you to determine the source(s) of your rule and to be content that the authorities you have chosen – whether constitutional, statutory, administrative, judicial, or some combination of these – provide the best support for that rule. If you are not convinced, additional research is likely necessary.

---

9. The format your "rule proof" should take will be explained more fully in Part 4 of this chapter. For now, you need to ensure that you have enough authority to prove the rule as you have conceived it.

3. Application

Once you have determined the likely issues and discovered the applicable rules, you are ready to consider how your facts apply to the relevant test(s). This section – sometimes termed "application" and sometimes termed "analysis" (although this book uses the term "analysis" to refer to the entire IRAC process) – is where you analyze whether your facts meet the stated rule. It is also where you directly compare and contrast your facts with the facts of the precedent cases you identified when determining the rule.

If one of your issues was a *legal* issue – for example, the law was unclear whether a renter, as opposed to a property owner, could sue another for nuisance – the bulk of your "thinking" occurs when trying to determine whether a renter may sue. Once the proper legal test is determined, the application is often straightforward. If a renter may sue and your client is a renter, then she may sue. If a renter may not sue and your client is a renter, then she may not sue. The "application" can be as simple as that with a legal issue.

Most issues, though, are not purely *legal*. They are also *factual*. Factual issues require more detailed application. In addition, when relevant case law exists, you should directly compare your facts and the facts of those relevant cases. Not all facts, however, are relevant (also called "material"). Consider the following example:

> Assume you are representing the defendant in a negligence action resulting from an automobile accident. The color of the plaintiff's car, even if disputed, is generally irrelevant and needs no discussion. However, assume the accident occurred when the defendant failed to yield to the plaintiff, but the plaintiff was driving a white car and there was a terrible blizzard at the time. Under these circumstances, the color of the plaintiff's car might very well be relevant.

You need to consider all facts and the parties' legal claims to determine what is a *relevant* fact.

When you have applicable case law (meaning the legal issue is the same as in your case), note the factual similarities and dissimilarities between each case and your case. The general rule is this: if a case has similar facts to your case, the result should be the same; if a case has dissimilar facts to your case, the result should be different. Of course, not every fact will be the same as (or different from) your case. Often, you will need to sift through the facts to determine which seemed most significant to the result. The court's *reasoning* will often assist in this endeavor.

a. Applying Facts to an "Elements" Test

With an elements test, each element that is potentially disputed becomes its own issue. Hence, you should use the IRAC framework to think through *each element*. Start by writing a list of all the elements, paying special attention to the connectors ("or" versus "and"). Next, taking one element at a time, move through the IRAC process (determining the issue, rule, application, and conclusion) for element 1, then determining the issue, rule, application, and conclusion for element 2, etc.[10]

b. Applying Facts to a "Factors" Test

With a factors test, it is generally very difficult to consider factors one at a time. Hence, the thought process discussed above when applying facts to an elements test will rarely be effective with a factors test. The reason is this: because a court will consider *all* of the factors together, isolating them does not give you the complete picture. You need to examine the "totality of the circumstances," not one factor at a time.

Begin by reviewing all of the authorities that reached a particular result. Which factors weighed in favor of the plaintiff?[11] Which

---

10. This organization will be discussed more fully in the context of outlining (see Part 3 of this chapter), but for now, just note that you need to think about these elements one at a time, not in the aggregate.

11. The term "plaintiff" is used generically here, referring to the same *type* of party. For example, consider all criminal defendants, for purposes of a *Miranda* challenge, as defendants (or plaintiffs, as long as you are consistent), re-

weighed in favor of the defendant? How strong – or weak – were the relative factors? Do the same for the cases that reached the opposite result. Then, think about your case. *On the whole*, are your facts more like the cases where the plaintiff won, or where the defendant won? Compare and contrast those facts in the aggregate, considering the relevant factors in reaching your result. But you can rarely check factors off a list the way you would with elements, as the facts in their *entirety* will be the relevant inquiry.

4. Conclusion

At last you have reached the easiest step in the thought process: the conclusion. If your rule is an elements test, go through your list of elements (which, you will recall, are sub-issues) and the results of your factual application for each element. If all necessary elements are met, the test is satisfied. If any necessary element is not met, the test is not satisfied. If your rule is a factors test, consider whether, overall, your case is more like the cases that found the rule was met or the cases that found the rule was not met. The conclusion is less important than the first three steps in the IRAC process; even if the reader disagrees with your conclusion, as long as the other steps are clear, he can reach his own conclusion.

Eventually, though, you will need to reach – and explicitly state – your conclusion on each issue. That conclusion may change, however, as you continually move through and between the various stages of the writing process. If you are ultimately drafting an "objective" document, such as an inner-office memorandum, keep an open mind about your conclusion and be willing to change it if the analysis suggests a different result. But at some point, you will need to conclude.

---

gardless of who is bringing the particular action and their actual titles in the cases; consider all landlords to be plaintiffs in forcible entry and detainer actions; etc.

BREAK IT DOWN, PART 2: RESEARCH

The world is formed from the void,
like utensils from a block of wood.
The Master knows the utensils,
yet keeps to the block:
thus she can use all things. – ch. 28

As with the writing process (of which research is one part), legal research is a process. It is also more than simply the search for information. Legal research is part of the analytical process in resolving legal disputes. Legal research is intricately connected to legal analysis, whether you are determining what to look for, pondering whether what you have found is relevant, or considering whether you need more.

Furthermore, legal research is not linear. It has numerous "steps," but you need to become proficient at moving between the various steps in a circular fashion. Sometimes, you will begin with secondary sources. Sometimes, you will begin with a controlling statute. Sometimes, you will begin with case law.

Regardless of where you begin, legal research is complex. But as with writing, it becomes much easier with practice. At this stage, keep in mind two important considerations. First, each problem and each researcher are unique, and the same path will not work for all projects or all people. Second, one key resource is frequently overlooked by students, judges, and practitioners: law librarians. Academic, courthouse, and firm reference librarians spend their lives helping people with research projects. They enjoy it, and they are good at it. As with all things, there is no need to reinvent the wheel. Ask for their help.

By now, you are probably proficient – at least relatively – at computerized legal research, and you should know the basics of manual legal research. But most legal researchers could be more efficient in their integration of print and computerized sources. This part will highlight various sources, identifying which are generally more effective in one format versus the other. It will also introduce (or refresh your memory on) some more advanced research topics.

1. Secondary Sources

Secondary sources, as contrasted with primary authority, are never binding. You generally won't cite secondary sources, unless you are addressing an issue of first impression or arguing for a change in the law. Because secondary sources summarize or comment on the law and provide citations to primary authority, however, they are often helpful.

Some legal researchers begin regularly with secondary sources, and some never use them. Whatever your inclinations, consider using them when you know little about an area or when researching an obscure area of the law. In those circumstances, secondary sources can both help you narrow your search as well as provide useful leads to primary authority. If you are familiar with the area of law or already have on-point primary authority, secondary source research may provide fewer benefits.

Assuming you have decided to review a secondary source, you will need to begin with a good list of search terms, as almost all secondary sources are navigated with an index of some sort. The next step is to select the most appropriate secondary source. Almost all secondary sources are available in print, although most are also now on-line. It is generally efficient to research secondary sources either in print or electronically.

When selecting a particular source, keep these points in mind. First, encyclopedias and nutshells provide a quick overview and can lead to additional search terms. They also can provide citations to primary authority. Even if case citations are not from your jurisdiction, the West digest topics and key numbers assigned to the case (discussed below) can help you find relevant cases within your jurisdiction. Second, law review articles are generally most helpful when you are trying to argue for what the law *should* be.

Third, American Law Reports (ALR's) are often useful when there are splits in authority; they catalog arguments on both sides and include sample cases. They are not exhaustive, but ALR's are often a helpful starting point. Fourth, treatises can be more persuasive than other secondary sources because their authors are generally well respected, and they *are* often cited. If you aren't sure whether a particular text is a treatise, ask a librarian. Fifth, don't forget continuing legal education (CLE) materials. They can also be very helpful. The difficulty is in finding them, as they are not well organized and generally do not have a good indexing system. But consider looking for on-point CLE materials if you are working on a narrow issue that is a hot topic in your jurisdiction. Your state or local bar association can generally put you in touch with those likely to know about the issue – CLE presenters – and the presenters are often willing to answer questions.

Finally, formbooks often provide a good starting point, but be sure to customize them for your particular purpose. Although commercial formbooks exist, the most common formbooks are those created within an office, such as a brief bank. If you have already drafted eleven motions to compel disclosure, you will likely save time by looking at those you drafted before. But be careful – you don't want to end up like the attorney who submitted a motion to suppress but forgot to change the defendant's name and many of the key facts. In addition, be sure your law is current and research to see if you can find support that is factually more on-point.

2. Primary Sources

Because primary sources are "the law," you will ultimately be searching for on-point primary sources from within your jurisdiction. Almost all primary sources are available in both print and electronic formats, and the most effective format varies depending on the type of authority and the particular project. Whether using print or electronic sources, begin your primary source search by looking in the smallest possible jurisdiction or in the smallest possible database. If you find nothing on-point, you can always expand your search.

With primary sources, always look first for a relevant constitutional or statutory provision. If one governs your situation, you will save hours by finding it early in the research process. If none governs, you can move on to other authorities. Look for constitutions and statutes using an index, whether searching in print or on-line. It is often easier to research annotated statutes in print, but if you are researching electronically, use the "book browse"/"next section" feature so you can see the sections before and after the section you find most on-point.

Pay special attention to definition and purpose sections and use the references provided by the publisher – statutory history information, references to regulations, notes of decisions (and the table of contents when they are lengthy), digest topics and key numbers, and secondary source citations. Be sure to update using *Shepard's* or *KeyCite*. Sheparding and KeyCiting are substantially more effective on-line than in print.

If you have a relevant statutory provision, and if the statutory language is ambiguous, you may also need to research legislative history. Legislative history is irrelevant if the statutory language is clear, but often there is no "plain meaning" and Congress' intent is relevant. Look for references to U.S.C.C.A.N. (United States Code Congressional and Administrative News) in the annotated code; committee reports can be weighty. Floor debates are less helpful, but sometimes useful. Look to see what the courts interpreting the statute relied upon, as that is often the most persuasive legislative history. Finally, if you are conducting state legislative history research, consult with a law librarian. It may be available on-line, although it is generally more difficult to obtain than federal legislative history.

In addition, look in the statute's annotations for any references to administrative regulations. Administrative materials are often not covered in basic legal research and writing courses, but they are sometimes essential to your research – and sometimes they are the easiest place to get the answer. Administrative regulations, for example, are rules passed by the agency charged with enforcing a statute. They usually provide more detail than the statute but are structured and look like a statute. It is much easier to research federal administrative regulations electronically, because the statutes have links directly to the regulations. The print format of the Code of Federal Regulations is updated once a year but in cycles, so the book you are reviewing can be up to nine months old.

Constitutions, statutes, and administrative regulations, even when relevant, will often not provide the complete answer to your problem. Interpretive case law (presuming a relevant statute) can help tremendously. The starting point for researching this case law is the annotated code – providing another reason to start your re-search by looking for a statute. If the annotations are incomplete, as they sometimes are, or if there is no controlling statute, follow these tips for finding relevant case law.

First, using your search terms, look in a digest – either in print or on-line – to find cases addressing your topic. Many researchers jump right to Lexis or Westlaw and type in a natural language query to find relevant cases. Although this strategy may be effective some of the time, it is unlikely to be effective all of the time, and it is gen-erally very inefficient.

Electronic word searching is generally under-inclusive. Computer searches can give the researcher the false sense that he has found all potentially relevant information. Even with *expert* researchers – law librarians – one study determined that when they executed com-puter searches, 80% of what they found was relevant, but they found only 20% of the relevant information. If the pros are only batting .200, it is unlikely we will do much better.[1]

Digest searching is substantially more effective. You likely had to look through print digests at some point in your legal research train-ing, but many researchers forget about this tool. Digests, which are essentially indices, are incredibly useful because they organize cases by subject, regardless of the particular words each individual judge used to express those concepts. In print, find the digest volumes for your jurisdiction (generally located right after or before the re-porters). Using your search terms, look in the descriptive word index to find relevant topics and key numbers. Next, take a relevant topic and key number and, using the main (not descriptive word index) digest volumes, look for the relevant topic name on the spine, and then look for your key number within that topic. The di-gest will give you summaries (digest entries) for each case in that ju-risdiction with a discussion on that topic. If you are working on-line, click on the hyperlink below the relevant topic and key number,

---

1. Daniel P. Dabney, "The Curse of Thamus: An Analysis of Full-Text Legal Document Retreival," 78 *L. Lib. J.* 5, 26 (1986).

specify the jurisdiction where you want to conduct the digest search, and review the case summaries.

The digest entries are helpful, but not sufficient. Be sure to read each case you intend to rely on and update your research with *Shepard's* or *KeyCite*. Also review cases cited in the relevant case law, as they are sometimes more helpful than the cases you initially found.

If possible, conduct digest searching in a West publication, whether in print or on-line; Lexis also has a digest system, but it does not currently have the breadth or depth of the West digest topic and key number system. Furthermore, cases are even easier to find if you already have a case on-point, even if it is from another jurisdiction. Using any on-point case, you can locate other cases on the same area of law by using the digest topic and key number that corresponds to the issue or issues you are researching; using that topic and key number, look in the digest for your jurisdiction to find cases on that same area of law.

In addition to judicial decisions, administrative agencies sometimes act (in addition to the rule-making/enforcement role discussed above) in an adjudicative role, creating their own body of case law. If you practice in an area governed by administrative law, be sure to check for this authority. Law librarians are helpful in this regard. Finally, the executive branch (whether federal or state) creates primary law by virtue of executive orders. You will generally have some references to an executive order prior to conducting research in this area.

3. Overall Considerations

Globally, you will be most effective and efficient at legal research if you do a few things. First, map out a research plan before you begin. Second, consider cost effectiveness between print and electronic research, including print cost, before you begin. Third, if you have not conducted manual legal research in some time (meaning you have not opened an actual book), try to complete your next project or two using only the books. Then, go back to the computer. Similarly, if you are one of the few who prefer to conduct almost all of your legal research manually, try completing a few projects using only the computer. Under either scenario, you will learn that there are advantages to each format, and you will soon become more comfortable moving between the two formats efficiently.

The best search for almost all projects involves a mix of print and electronic sources. Learning when to use each is essential for efficient research. Regardless of whether you are using print sources, electronic sources, or a combination of the two, expect to run into some glitches. Allocate more time for the research phase than you think you will need at the outset. Furthermore, move freely between the various secondary and primary sources. Don't try to march in a line, thinking once you have looked for secondary sources (or primary sources) you are done with that task. The sources all connect and they all lead to each other. Use those connections – statutory annotations, digest topic and key numbers, cross-references to regulations, links within authorities, *Shepard's/KeyCite*, etc. not just to update, but to *find new sources*. When you keep running across the same sources, your research is likely comprehensive.

BREAK IT DOWN, PART 3: OUTLINE

The simplest pattern is the clearest. – ch. 65

Once you have some preliminary ideas about your project, you can – and should – create a basic outline. Your outline can (and likely will) change throughout the legal writing process, but having some form of an outline makes it much more likely that your ultimate written product will be better both analytically and organizationally. Furthermore, outlining as a precursor to actually writing helps you identify areas of confusion before you draft the entire document, saving you time in the end by minimizing the need for substantive revision.

Outlines help show the relationships between concepts. Is one issue a sub-issue of another, or its own independent issue? Must you demonstrate all three elements to prevail, or will any one of the three suffice? Without an outline, these questions may remain unanswered – for you, and for the reader.

Many writers have difficulty outlining and they therefore skip this step. Although some documents are effective even though the writer did not create some form of an outline, chances are good that the document could have been even better if the writer had completed this step. If you have always had difficulty outlining, try outlining a document you have already written. Do the connections make sense? Is the order logical? After you have outlined a few documents you wrote previously, try drafting a *short* – one page or less – outline for a document you are working on currently. With practice, your outlining skills can improve. In the end, this step should make your writing process more efficient and more effective.

Many writers who have difficulty outlining struggle because they are not linear thinkers. If you are a non-linear thinker, beginning with another structure, such as a bubble diagram, may help. But most legal readers are linear thinkers, and they generally expect legal analysis to be conveyed in a linear fashion. A traditional outline will go a long way toward structuring your written product linearly.

Begin with a very general and short outline and, depending on the size of the project, add detail over time. If your ultimate document is a three-page memorandum, two points written at the top of a page may suffice for an outline. If you are drafting a forty-page appellate brief, on the other hand, you will likely need an outline that is at least a page or two long.[1]

1. Creating an Effective Outline

First, generally *organize your outline around the issues* – and if the rule has them, the rule's elements – rather than around cases or other sources. Your legal analysis followed the IRAC format,[2] and your outline should do the same. If your written document is organized around the authorities rather than the issues, it will read like a book report – perhaps interesting, but not very helpful in solving the legal problem. Your reader will rely on you to identify the issues and resolve each in turn, using synthesized authorities to support your conclusions.

Second, *decide which issues or elements should go first, second, third,* and so on. You generally have some flexibility, with a few exceptions. First, procedural issues should almost always be addressed before substantive issues. Second, legal issues should generally be addressed before factual issues. Third, address threshold issues first (meaning those issues that could eliminate the remainder of the analysis depending on their outcome), but still address the other issues unless there is no chance they will survive. Aside from these general guidelines, if you have a relevant statute, it can often provide a logical structure for your outline. You can follow the ordering of elements by the legislature or regroup them if doing so seems more logical or more persuasive.

Finally, *within each section, follow basic IRAC format.* What is your issue? Briefly, what is the governing rule (with citations)? Which facts are relevant, grouped by those that favor (and then disfavor) a particular result? What is the likely conclusion?

---

1. This book began with a one-page outline that became progressively more detailed; as I filled in the outline, I constantly revised it to avoid repetition and to clarify the relationships between concepts.

2. Issue, Rule, Application, Conclusion; see Chapter 4, Part 1.

2. Outlining Options

If your issue has sub-issues – for example, when a statute has elements and more than one is questionable in your case – address each with a separate IRAC. These separate IRAC's will generally fit within the Application section of your main IRAC on that issue. Using the earlier shoplifting statute from Part 1 of this chapter – "It is illegal for a person to take property without paying from a place of business when the property is marked for sale," modified by the state supreme court's holding in *Jones* that in order to violate this statute, the defendant "must intend to permanently deprive the business of the property" – assume these facts. You are the prosecutor, and the defendant is charged with violating that statute. The defendant went into Target and purchased a CD. At the checkout stand, he wrote a check using a pen on the counter. But rather than putting the pen back, he placed it in his pocket and walked out of the store. Is the defendant likely to be convicted?

An outline for this memo may look something like the one on the facing page. Note that the sub-issues fit within the application section of the main IRAC. Note also that these sub-issues come directly from the elements – one from the statute itself, and one from a court interpretation. Buzz words make it clear to the reader that the writer is simply following the language of the rule. In addition, the conclusion on the "intent to permanently deprive" issue could reasonably go either way, depending on how the writer formulated the rule from *Jones*. If the writer concluded that there likely was an intent to permanently deprive, the final conclusion would be altered as well to reflect that change.

These "mini-IRAC's" will vary in length. Some may require in-depth analysis to determine the likely rule. Some may be short – like the "pen marked for sale," as that is merely a factual question and we do not have all the necessary information. Some will be longer because there are a great deal of relevant facts and a fair amount of case law for comparison purposes. Although the example above is short and has few facts, facts may appear in more than one section, because the same fact may be relevant to more than one issue or sub-issue.

I: Defendant (D) guilty of SL?
R: person commits SL when:
    1) takes property
    2) without paying
    3) from place of business
    4) property marked for sale; and
    5) with intent to permanently deprive
A: 1) – 3) clearly met. D took the pen, he didn't pay, and Target is a business.

> **Mini-IRAC:** I: pen "marked for sale"?
> **#1**   R: (no further rule – just main one – so omit here)
>   A: facts don't say. Need more info.
>   C: unclear. Need to investigate.

> **Mini-IRAC:** I: "intent to permanently deprive"?
> **#2**   R: intent to perm. depr. requires conscious action. *Jones.* In *Jones*, Jones shopping & 3-yr.-old son put candy bar in Jones' coat pocket without him knowing. Jones charged w/ SL. Ct. held no SL b/c no "intent to perm. deprive."
>   A: like Jones, whose son put candy bar in his pocket, D likely put pen in his pocket unknowingly/ was unaware he was taking it. Possibly just out of habit. However, unlike in *Jones*, where intervening 3rd party (son), here D put pen in his own pocket. But still likely not conscious action.
>   C: likely had no intent to perm deprive

C: even if pen marked for sale, likely not SL b/c likely no intent to perm. deprive

Note also the boxes drawn around each IRAC – the main IRAC and each mini-IRAC. These boxes in your outline can help ensure you are following the IRAC structure. Furthermore, some readers will not expect you to repeat information from a main IRAC within a mini-IRAC. For example, there is no "sub-rule" defining when a pen is marked for sale. Within that mini-IRAC, some readers would expect you to omit the "R" and jump directly from the Issue (whether the pen was marked for sale) to the Application (the absence of facts on this sub-issue). Other readers will expect (or permit) you to repeat the Rule from the main IRAC. As with all other aspects of writing, if you know your audience's preferences, follow them. If not, use your best judgment about what makes the document read most clearly.

If you had a two-issue problem (as opposed to one issue that had two sub-issues), your outline could be structured as follows:

> I:
> R:
> A:
> C:
>
> I:
> R:
> A:
> C:

If you have one issue, but it involves three factors rather than elements, your outline could look like this:

> I:
> R:
> A:
> C:

Returning to our *Miranda* example, where the rule contains two elements, and one of the elements contains factors, your outline could look like this:

I: confession without warnings admissible?
R: suppress if:
   1) custodial; and
   2) interrogation (*Miranda*)
A:

> **Mini-IRAC** I: custodial?
> **# 1**   R: state factors (1, 2, 3, & 4)
>   cases A – D: custodial b/c....
>   cases E – G: not custodial b/c ...
>   A: our case more like A – D b/c ...
>   C: hence, likely custodial

> **Mini-IRAC** I: interrogation?
> **# 2**   R: ___? Proof?
>   A: ___?
>   C: ___?

C: B/c likely custodial and likely interrogation, the confession is likely inadmissible

Whatever format you use, outlining prior to drafting the ultimate document will likely result in a more effective final document.

BREAK IT DOWN, PART 4: WRITE

*Express yourself completely,
then keep quiet. – ch. 23*

This section addresses writing the "meat" of any paper – the discussion section of a memorandum, the argument section of a motion, etc. Chapter 2 addresses the format expectations for various documents, including the particular sections expected.

Throughout the "writing" step, you need to constantly reevaluate your analysis. Generally, your initial analysis will change, at least somewhat, by the time you finish the written product. Do not fight this change. Do not resist the urge to rethink the problem. Do not refuse to go back into the library. Although these tasks may add some time, they are likely to result in a greatly improved written product. Once the outline is drafted, however, the "writing" becomes easier – although it still may not be easy.

If you have thought, researched, and outlined – a number of times, with revised conclusions – by the time you get to the "writing" stage, you have already begun writing. The outline is written work product, and perhaps the most significant. But now you need to finish the paper. Below are three tips to help you put pen to paper (or fingers to keyboard).

1. Break Through Writer's Block

Many good writers fail to fulfill their potential because they somehow cannot force the words onto paper. We often put off the most difficult tasks, including writing; many writers research until there is insufficient time to draft a quality document. Others sit at a blank computer screen, literally paralyzed. Still others start draft after draft, discarding each after a few pages because it is not perfect. The three suggestions below should help eliminate, or at least reduce, writer's block.

First, start typing earlier than you think you need to, and remind yourself regularly of your reason for writing this particular document. Whether you have a court deadline, a course deadline, or a self-imposed deadline because you have other projects that need attention, you need to write sooner rather than later. Aim to finish early; if you are successful, you have some time off. If not, you are more likely to still complete it on time. And whether the ultimate benefit is a good grade or winning a case, what you are doing matters. Let that motivate you to begin writing and to continue writing.

Second, sit down at the computer, turn off the monitor, and start typing. Type for at least fifteen minutes before turning on the screen.[1] For those of us who are perfectionists, this allows us to write without second-guessing – and deleting – every word. Much of writer's block can be eliminated this way. Third, start typing something you know well, such as the "Facts" section (discussed in Chapter 2). This way, you get the easier part done first, and once you are in the flow of writing, you can move to a more difficult part or section.

2. Follow Your Outline/Structure

Depending on the level of detail in your outline, "writing" can be as simple as making complete sentences out of phrases. Even with a more basic outline, use your outline as the guide for your structure. Main outline headings will become point headings in your written document; sub-issues in the outline will become sub-headings in your written document, etc. As you write, though, follow these suggestions to move from your outline – the expression of your thinking stage – to the communication of your analysis to the reader.

a. Moving from IRAC to CRuPAC

Although we analyze and initially outline a problem using IRAC, when we draft the actual document we generally shift to an organizational structure better represented by this acronym: CRuPAC.[2]

---

1. This suggestion was made by Chief Justice Rebecca Berch of the Arizona Supreme Court during an appellate advocacy class.
2. This paradigm is discussed in detail in Richard K. Neumann, Jr., *Legal Reasoning and Legal Writing: Structure, Strategy, and Style* 91–102 (6th ed., Aspen 2009). Although he does not use the acronym CRuPAC, he suggests adopting a structure that can be represented in this way. Following CRuPAC

C = Conclusion
Ru = Rule
P = Proof of the Rule
A = Application
C = Conclusion

Many writers find it helpful to create a template on their computer with these letters in the margins. They can then fill in each part (C, Ru, P, A, and C), one at a time, ensuring their organization will be clear.[3] Each of these parts will be discussed, but note this is only one minor change – Issue to Conclusion – and one explicit addition – Proof of the Rule – although the Proof was already introduced when discussing the Rule.[4]

i. Conclusion

First, legal readers generally expect the written analysis – especially in persuasive writing – to begin with your *conclusion* on each issue rather than a mere statement of the issue. This change is simple; for each IRAC and mini-IRAC, take your conclusion, rephrase it, and begin your IRAC with that rather than an issue statement. The conclusion for each issue becomes your heading.

Furthermore, most conclusions in objective memos are somewhat qualified – "likely," "probably," etc. – because in the law, rarely is the expected result in any given case guaranteed. Qualification is permissible and, at least in law school, generally expected. But a conclusion that simply states, "our client *may* prevail," does the reader little good, as that is almost always true. What the reader is looking for from you – the writer – is whether it is *likely* that our client will prevail. Be sure to provide a credible prediction about the likely outcome.

---

for law school or bar exams is not, though, recommended; it is not necessary, and can often be a detriment on exams. IRAC is more effective for exams.

3. CRuPAC is the organizational framework for the discussion section in a memorandum and the argument section in a motion or brief. See Chapter 2(B)(1)(b)(iv), (5)(b), and (6)(b).

4. See Chapter 4, Part 1.

ii. Rule

As noted in Part 1 of this chapter, the rule should be a synthesized statement of the law that governs your issue. It can come from a constitution, a statute, an administrative regulation, an executive order, or a case (or any combination of these). If your rule comes from a statute-like authority (including constitutions and other rules), quote the relevant language. If your rule comes from a case, state the rule in your own words, but keep the court's "buzz words" for key concepts/elements.

iii. Proof

Legal readers are a skeptical bunch. They tend to distrust that which is not proven. Hence, it is your job to not only conduct sound legal analysis, but to demonstrate to your reader that you have done so. This requires that you not only clearly synthesize and state the governing rules, but that you *prove* them by adequately describing the authority that supports the rule.

Fortunately, with statutes, proving the rule is easy: quote the relevant portion of the statute and provide the citation. This suffices to "prove" the rule.[5] With cases, though, rule proof requires more. Quotes are like statistics; you can almost always find one to say what you want, even if it is not the rule of the case. Hence, quotations from cases are generally not all that helpful.

Furthermore, the reader is unlikely to accept at face value your formulation of the rule from a case without knowing at least three important things: its facts, the issue, and its holding (and the rationale if that is helpful to the analysis, as it often is). Hence, for every case you cite as support for a rule, generally include these components. If the case is not overly significant, you may be able to do this in a parenthetical. If the case is key, you may need a para-

---

5. As noted in earlier in this chapter, however, the bare statutory language alone rarely provides "the complete answer"; some consideration of case law is generally required even with a statutorily-based issue. See Chapter 4, Part 2, section 2.

graph or more to describe the case and adequately prove the rule. As with the rule itself, generally summarize or paraphrase (especially with facts) rather than quote from cases. Remember to focus on the relevant facts, clearly state the issue, and describe the holding, including the court's action. For example, did the court reverse the defendant's conviction? If so, the reader is far more likely to believe your rule statement that particular confessions are inadmissible. The court's judgment, along with the key facts and the issue, help convince the reader that your rule is in fact accurate. Consider the following example:

> Returning to our shoplifting example, assume you phrased your synthesized rule as follows: "It is illegal for a person to take property without paying from a place of business when the property is marked for sale" when the defendant intends to "permanently deprive" the business of that property. (Note the statutory language is quoted and the case holding is paraphrased, but includes the buzz words.) The proof would then look like this:
>
> Ariz. Rev. Stat. Ann. § 13-1801 (West 2009); *Pleasantville v. Jones*, 928 P.2d 357, 360 (Ariz. 2003). In *Jones*, the defendant was shopping in Safeway with his three-year old son, Jacob. 928 P.2d at 358. Jacob took a $.49 candy bar off a rack near the cashier stand while the defendant placed groceries on the counter. Jacob then put the candy bar in the defendant's coat pocket. The defendant did not know his son had picked up the candy bar or placed it in his pocket. *Id.* Jones was charged with shoplifting and convicted at trial. *Id.* The Arizona Supreme Court reversed Jones' conviction, holding that he was not guilty because he did not "intend to permanently deprive" Safeway of the candy bar. *Id.* at 360.

iv. Application

Directly comparing and contrasting our facts with the facts of precedent cases is key here. This section is often introduced with statements such as "in our case," or "here, ...". You should generally avoid statements of pure fact (unrelated to an underlying element of your rule); instead, directly tie your facts to the legal test to demonstrate why facts are relevant and what the result should be. An exception exists when the first sentence of a short application states the rule combined with facts.

When conducting case comparisons, be explicit. Compare or contrast the underlying *facts* of the case, not just the legal conclusion. Consider the following example:

> Assume your client, O'Connor, has been sued for breach of contract for failing to deliver 100,000 pounds of grapes to a wine manufacturer. His grape crop, however, was completely destroyed by wildfires. Assume the contract is silent as to whether this constitutes a valid defense. Assume also that a controlling case named *Smith* held a supplier had a defense and was not liable for breach of contract despite failing to deliver lettuce, when flooding completely destroyed his lettuce crop.
>
> The following "application" is insufficient: "Like in *Smith*, O'Connor has a defense." Although the reader is made aware that you think there is a similarity between *Smith* and our case, the factual similarity is not made clear. Instead, compare *facts*:
>
> > "Like in *Smith*, where the defendant's lettuce crop was completely destroyed by flooding, O'Connor's grape crops were completely destroyed by wildfires."
>
> Note that the facts are not *identical* – but the type of crop is not likely determinative, and both crop losses were caused by natural forces. Hence, the facts are very likely sufficiently analogous to require the same result.

By comparing the underlying facts, you are much more likely to reach (and to convince your reader you have reached) valid conclusions.

v. Conclusion

After all the steps above, the conclusion is relatively straightforward. Be as definitive as you can, but generally qualify your conclusion with "likely" or "probably."

b. Depth of Analysis

Probably the most common question writers ask is: "how long should this be?" That is always a difficult question, and the most common answer is probably, "as long as it needs to be to answer the question." More concretely, under some circumstances, an entire CRuPAC can fit into one paragraph. Sometimes, one CRuPAC can be thirty pages or more.

Although the conclusion and rule statement are generally short, the rule proof and application sections are what usually create longer documents. The more contested a point, and the more central that point to ultimate success, the more space, in general, you will need. Rule proof, for example, can range from a simple statutory citation or case citation and parenthetical explanation to several paragraphs or pages discussing a case's facts, issue, holding, and rationale in detail. The application can range from a sentence (as with a "legal issue") to several paragraphs or even pages. And recall that CRuPAC's can contain mini-CRuPAC's, making the main CRuPAC relatively long.

c. Overview Paragraphs

Once you have written your analysis (your CRuPAC or CRu-PAC's), go back and think about how to help your reader earlier in the document. For longer documents especially, beginning with an "overview paragraph" (also called a "road map paragraph" or an "umbrella paragraph") can help the reader understand the basic analysis before reading the entire document. The overview paragraph should show relationships between various issues; for example, can the plaintiff pursue two theories of liability in the alternative? Or are they mutually exclusive? Is one claim dependent upon another? In short, use the overview paragraph to educate your reader without the detail of your entire analysis.

d. Thesis Statements

Just as the document should begin with an overview, each section and each paragraph should begin with a strong statement that summarizes the point of that section or paragraph. These statements –

often called "thesis statements" – are akin to topic sentences, but they differ in one significant respect. Thesis statements are probative – that is, they advance a position, rather than merely describing a topic.[6] In persuasive writing especially, thesis statements are essential.

If you use the CRuPAC format and write using your outline, you likely already have a thesis statement for each section – the heading, which is also the first Conclusion (the first "C"). Conclusions are classic thesis statements. But even at the paragraph level, using thesis statements will both strengthen your writing and help the reader understand your arguments more clearly. Especially with precedent cases, consider starting paragraphs with the point of the case rather than "in case X,...." or worse yet: "In 1960, the court decided Case Y." Instead, begin with the *reason* you are using the case:

> Whether the defendant's freedom was significantly restricted, whether the police threatened him, and whether the defendant asked to leave are three of the relevant factors in determining if a defendant was "in custody" for Miranda purposes. *Maine v. Thibodeau*, 475 U.S. 1144, 1146 (1986).

In a well written legal document, the reader should be able to read your overview paragraph, the headings, and the first sentence of every paragraph and completely understand your argument. If the reader cannot, add thesis statements and ensure your paragraphs are internally consistent with that thesis.

3. Think about Your Writing Style[7]

For centuries, legal writing was convoluted and full of jargon. The Plain English movement is changing that, and the vast major-

---

6. One colleague refers to thesis statements as "topic sentences on steroids."

7. Several texts are devoted entirely to legal writing style, including: Anne Enquist and Laurel Currie Oates, *Just Writing: Grammar, Punctuation, and Style for the Legal Writer* (3d ed., Aspen 2009); Bryan A. Garner, *The Redbook: A Manual on Legal Style* (2d ed., Thomson-West 2006); Terri LeClerq, *Guide to*

ity of readers agree it is for the better. Simplicity is now the expectation. Your reader – regardless of who that may be – is incredibly busy, and she will not want to spend more time reading than necessary. If your document is difficult to understand and sections need to be reread, the reader will be unhappy. Similarly, if your document is repetitive and longer than necessary, the reader will be unhappy.

Many texts and a major survey suggest the two most significant style requirements are clarity and conciseness.[8] Of course, these goals often conflict; with more explanation, the reader is more likely to be clear about your point. However, you are less likely to be concise. Know that these dual goals are sometimes at odds, and that clarity ultimately trumps conciseness. But be as concise as you can while being clear.

The single easiest way for most writers to be more concise is to use active voice. With active voice, the sentence follows this basic pattern: subject, verb, object. For example, "John kicked the ball" is a classic active-voice sentence. The passive version of that sentence, "the ball was kicked by John," is one-third longer. Unless your point is to emphasize the ball, there is no reason to use the extra words and to make the reader wait until the end of the sentence to picture the actor – John – completing the act. In addition to being substantially longer, this "object-verb-subject" structure creates a less vivid picture for the reader.[9]

Legal Writing Style (4th ed., Aspen 2007); and Richard Wydick, *Plain English for Lawyers* (5th ed., Carolina Academic Press 2005). I suggest all legal writers get a good style book and keep it handy as a reference.

8. *See, e.g.,* Charles R. Calleros, *Legal Method & Writing* 239 (5th ed., Aspen 2006); Susan Hanley Kosse and David T. ButleRitchie, "How Judges, Practitioners, and Legal Writing Teachers Assess the Writing Skills of New Law Graduates: A Comparative Study," 53 *J. Leg. Educ.* 80, 84 (2003).

9. Of course, if you have a valid reason for ignoring the actor, use passive voice. For example, if your client robbed a bank, the statement "John robbed the bank" is not very helpful to your case. The ultimate passive voice sentence – one that only implies the actor – would serve you best: "The bank was robbed." Use passive voice when it makes sense to do so, but not as a default position.

Another way to be concise is to avoid repetition. A good outline will help avoid structural repetition. Additionally, review your writing to ensure your points are clear, but not needlessly repeated. CRuPAC inherently includes some repetition, but the one-sentence conclusion is often helpful to reiterate and it does not take much space. If you catch yourself beginning a sentence with "as stated before," or "again," ask yourself if you *really* need to state it again.

With persuasive writing especially, keep in mind two basic principles: start with your strongest point, and use more detail to emphasize a point. Primacy and recency suggest readers will remember your first and last points; legal readers expect your most significant point to be first. So – unless some other reason dictates a different order – begin with your strongest argument, bury weaker arguments in the middle, and end on a somewhat strong argument. Similarly, bury negative facts and authorities in the middle of an issue, but use vivid detail to help draw attention and encourage the reader to remember favorable points. Use broad characterizations, on the other hand, to deemphasize a point.

Finally, one point about clarity is worth noting. It is far easier to read and understand a document with headings (and sub-headings, if the document is long) than one without. Clearly identify the different document sections (see Chapter 2), and make your conclusions for each CRuPAC (and mini-CRuPAC) headings (and sub-headings). Your reader will appreciate *the way* you have simplified her task.

BREAK IT DOWN, PART 5: REVISE

When he makes a mistake, he realizes it.
Having realized it, he admits it.
Having admitted it, he corrects it. – ch. 61

As you move freely between the various stages of the legal writing process, revising is the one you will return to most often. You will revise your thinking. You will revise your research. You will revise your outline. You will revise your writing. And you will likely do each of these things a number of times.

An effective writing process requires that you critically and continually evaluate your analysis and your communication of that analysis. You therefore need to think expressly about revising, rather than simply correcting typographical errors identified by spellcheck. Furthermore, you need to begin to revise more than a few hours before the document is due. True revision takes time, but the resulting work product is worth it.

A. What Does it Mean to "Critically Evaluate" a Piece of Writing?

To "critically evaluate" requires that you both *revise* and *polish* your writing. This is often referred to simply as "revising," but they are separated here to make it clear that both are necessary, and both are part of critically evaluating your work product.

Before addressing these two tasks in more detail, it is important to recognize that successful revision and polishing requires that we fill two roles – that of writer and that of reader. Although often very difficult, removing yourself from the "writer" role and placing yourself in the "reader" role will help tremendously with the revision process. Human nature is such that we generally think what we have written is good – even if it could be better. In legal writing, keep in mind that your audience is generally very skeptical; the reader is often someone you are trying to persuade, and even if you are communicating your "objective" analysis, the reader must agree with you.

To help you take on the "reader" role, as you read through a document – whether one you wrote or one drafted by a colleague – review the document as if you were the intended audience. If the ultimate reader is a judge who will know little or nothing about the dispute, ask yourself whether the document provides enough context for you to understand the problem. If the audience is expected to know a great deal about the problem, ask whether the document includes unnecessary detail. Keeping this "reader" perspective while both revising and polishing will help you identify problems you might otherwise miss.

1. Revising

Revising is the process of actually changing the substance of the document. Although it is incredibly important, few writers spend the amount of time necessary to truly *revise* a document. Instead, they hope that *polishing* it – even if what existed in the first place was unusable – will make the document satisfactory. Our instinct is to make the "easy" changes – those identified by another, those that involve cutting and pasting, and those that involve correcting citation, grammar, punctuation, and formatting. But that isn't enough.

Most readers will want clear organization, understandable and helpful thesis statements, headings, and solid analysis supported by authority. Without revision, the major and analytical problems that often exist in a first draft continue. Those problems surface in the writing process, and are rarely resolved completely in the first draft. Thus, a thorough *revision* is essential to having an effective document. True revision is rarely quick, but this necessary step will make a significant difference in the final product.

The first draft of any document should be thought of just as that – a draft. Submitting that draft to a professor, a partner, or a judge is not wise. Even if a first draft receives a good grade or results in a favorable outcome, the document almost always could have been *better* with even minimal revision.[1]

---

1. For example, when writing this book, I struggled with Chapter 4. For some reason, the first draft of that chapter didn't work. I spent months attempting to revise it – by cutting, pasting, rewriting, etc. – but it still did not work. I finally realized that the basic structure was not effective, and that the only way to make the chapter better was to cut it completely and start over. Although that was incredibly painful to do after putting so much time and en-

At the revision stage, if you find organizational problems, review your outline (or create one). You can often spot – and correct – organizational difficulties much easier at this global level. On the other hand, if a particular point does not seem to be supported, look for more support – and if none exists, omit the argument unless it is essential to your success.

2. Polishing

Polishing involves correcting obvious mistakes and "cleaning up" the document. Polishing is necessary, even though it does little to improve the underlying substance of the document. Although it may seem like needless form over substance, most readers believe that if the writing is sloppy, then the substance and analysis are suspect. Therefore, every writer should take the short amount of time necessary to polish a document, even if the reader is likely to be forgiving. As writers, it is very difficult to catch mistakes. And even as *readers*, we often miss many errors. Be sure to review your writing critically at this stage.

B. What about *Me* Will Help – & Hurt – in the Critical Evaluation Process?

Are you a big picture person? Or a detail person? Knowing this from the outset will help significantly when reviewing a document. Some readers will catch every misplaced comma, spelling error, and citation problem. Others will miss all of these issues, but notice that the first two global sections in a document should be switched for maximum effectiveness. The first is a detail person, and the second a big picture person.

---

ergy into it, selecting the entire chapter and hitting "delete" was an essential step in revising this book. Of course, everything that bothered me about the old Chapter 4 helped me to figure out a better structure and content for the new Chapter 4. In short, although it is difficult to scrap a chunk of work, it is sometimes necessary for effective revision.

Some readers know which they are; every time they read, they cannot help but correct detail mistakes, or they do not notice the details at all. Other readers may not be as aware of their natural tendencies. There are a few methods to help determine which type of reader you likely are. One easy way is to review a document and see what jumps out at you. This may answer the question for you quickly. If that does not help, think of a common occurrence to help you figure out your leanings. For example, are you the type of person who writes down every banking transaction and then immediately balances the checkbook, to the penny, the day the statement arrives? Or do you just have a general sense of "about how much" you have in the bank? If you are the former, you are likely a detail person, and if the latter, you are likely a big picture person.

A few folks are neither big picture nor detail people; they tend to see both, or neither, types of problems. For those readers with a more balanced perspective, no one type of problem seems paramount. Furthermore, it is not *better* to be a "big picture" person or a "detail" person. They are just different. But knowing your inherent tendencies helps tremendously when reviewing written documents.

If you are a detail person, read the document through once noting the detail problems, such as spelling, spacing, writing style, citation, and format errors. Then, reread the document, but this time paying special attention to the document outline, the thesis statements, and other global structural issues. For the detail person, it is often helpful to outline the document – even after it is written – to review the overall structural content and organization.

If you are a big picture person, read the document through, noting all the global problems and the questions you have as a reader. Then, go through the document several times, focusing each time on a separate detail issues – citation during the first round, grammar the second, spelling on the third, etc., until you have reviewed the document for all potential errors. For some readers, especially when reviewing their own documents, reading the paper backwards, sentence by sentence, helps them spot detail mistakes.

C. How Can I be Better at Revising and Polishing?

Probably the single best aid is to *leave ample time between writing and revising*. If you can put the document down for a few days, you will be able to review it with fresh eyes and a fresh mind, and the final product is likely to be substantially better than the first draft. However, in both law school and in practice, external deadlines often prohibit this kind of revision schedule. When that happens, still give yourself as much time as possible, knowing you will very likely need more time than you expect to revise. But don't wait until an hour before the document is due to review it; you will very likely be unhappy with the final product.

For structural revisions, consider using a *self-graded draft*. One type of self-graded draft uses different colored highlighters for each portion of the analysis.[2] For many writers, especially visual learners, using colors to highlight different sections of the CRuPAC will help identify problems with the document's organization. In addition, don't expect you will inherently know the solution to every problem. Just like researching legal issues, you may need to research writing issues. Good lawyers aren't distinguished because they know all the answers; they are distinguished because they can find – or create – the answers. Similarly, revising and polishing your writing is as much about reviewing the appropriate resources as it is about knowing the rules. Get a good style manual, and keep it on your desk.[3] Look up problems as they arise. Over time, you will need to review the manual less – but you will still need it. Also review a citation manual.[4] Proper citation format is expected, so take the time to ensure that your citations comply with an accepted format.

---

2. Mary Beth Beazley, "The Self-Graded Draft: Teaching Students to Revise Using Guided Self-Critique," 3 *Leg. Writing* 175 (1997).

3. See Chapter 4, Part 4, n.5 for a list of style manuals.

4. Currently, the two most accepted citation manuals are the *ALWD Citation Manual: A Professional System of Citation* (3rd ed., Aspen 2006) and *The Bluebook: A Uniform System of Citation* (18th ed., Harv. L. Rev. Assn. 2005). *ALWD* generally uses the same rules as the *Bluebook* (with a few minor excep-

Finally, show your writing to others, but only after at least a first revision yourself. And if you can, show the *outline* to others. A partner, a professor, or a colleague can often provide feedback at the structural stage, and that can save significant time later. Be sure, though, that you comply with all ethical rules, honor codes, and course requirements when seeking input on your writing.

In thinking, keep to the simple. – ch. 8

---

tions). The rules in *ALWD* tend to be more clearly stated, and it contains numerous examples. Recent editions of the *Bluebook* have improved; more examples have been added, and some controversial rules have been modified. However, the *Bluebook* is designed primarily for law review editors and others completing scholarly writing projects. It uses different typefaces and has different rules for academic and practical writing, and the *Bluebook* can therefore be cumbersome for practical writing projects. The rules and examples in the *ALWD Citation Manual* are in proper format for practitioners.

CHAPTER 5: KNOW WHEN TO STOP

The Master does his job
and then stops. – ch. 30

To be an effective writer, you need to know your – and your reader's – limits. We've all heard the speech that went on one minute (or one hour) too long. For example, President Lincoln spoke at Gettysburg for less than three minutes, following a speech that lasted for over two hours.[1] Yet the 272 word Gettysburg Address lives on and Edward Everett's speech has been long forgotten.

In writing, as with speeches, less is often more. And knowing when to stop is especially critical for effective legal writing. Legal readers are busy. They may not read past the first few pages, especially if you have not made your point by then. In addition to writing more concisely (discussed in Chapter 4, Part 4), consciously consider which arguments to raise, which authorities to rely on, and which comparisons to make – and which to leave out. "Shotgunning," where the writer essentially throws every conceivable argument at the wall to see what sticks, is rarely effective.

Instead, think about what is most likely to be persuasive (if drafting a persuasive document) or of concern to the reader (if drafting an objective document), as well as what is essential to include. Although you should err on the side of over-inclusiveness, be conservative in your judgment and, especially with persuasive documents, consider the likely effects on overall persuasiveness.

Hence, this Chapter will stop here.

Knowing when to stop,
you can avoid any danger. – ch. 32

---

1. Larry M. Boyle, "Legal Masterpieces: The Giants of American Law," 46 *Advoc.* 26, 28 (Sept. 2003).

CHAPTER 6: REFLECT

Knowing others is intelligence;
knowing yourself is true wisdom.
Mastering others is strength;
mastering yourself is true power. – ch. 33

We can all learn from our past experiences. As with most other endeavors, writing is a lifelong learning process. You are likely to become a better writer the more you write; thinking about it and actually "doing" it are incredibly effective tools for improving any skill. But your writing will improve significantly if you take the time after completing writing projects to reflect on what worked, what did not, and how it could be better. At times, you can gain at least some level of feedback directly: was the writing successful in meeting its goals? If you drafted a motion, did you prevail? If you drafted a letter to your client, did the client call to complain or ask questions, or did the client instead express an understanding of the situation and her options? If you drafted a memorandum for a legal writing class, what grade did you earn?

Of course, not all writings can be evaluated this way; for example, if you drafted a contract, even if it was signed, you would have to wait years to be sure that the contract properly anticipated and dealt with potential problems and that it was not challenged in court. Furthermore, sometimes a losing case is simply a losing case, and the best advocacy in the world cannot alter the inevitable. However, ignoring the outcome that resulted from a document you wrote will rarely help you become a better writer.

In addition, you can often ask for feedback on the effectiveness of your writing, even if the document is finalized. In law practice, for example, you can ask others in your office to review documents. You can also ask other valued mentors – judges, legal writing professors, or others, including peers.[1] The goal here is not the same as the goal when showing someone your outline or early draft – where you hope to improve *that* document. Rather, the goal here is to learn from what you wrote and to apply those lessons as you draft *new* documents.

---

1. Be conscious of ethical requirements, though, especially restrictions on sharing client confidences.

Furthermore, if the document was revised by someone else after it left your hands, how does your draft compare with the final version? What changes were analytical? What changes were organizational? What changes were technical? What can you learn about these changes that will help you be a better writer next time?

Take all advice, though, with a grain of salt. Two readers will not perceive the same strengths and weaknesses with the same document, just as two jurors will not always reach the same result after hearing the same evidence. However, each reader's reaction is important, and if several readers have similar reactions, you should take heed, even if you disagree. With legal writing, after the document leaves your hands, it is more about the reader than about you. The reader's reactions are what matter in the end; you may believe you have written the best document ever, but if the reader disagrees and the document is not effective, you are still likely to lose.

And in those instances when you cannot obtain feedback from another, review your final work product a few days, or even weeks, after it is completed. Look at the document with a critical eye: does it work? If you were the intended audience, would you be convinced of your conclusions? How could it be improved? If you received this as a draft from someone else, what would you change?

The goal with any recurring process is to learn from your mistakes so that you can avoid them next time. For example, do you routinely receive feedback that your organizational structure makes your documents difficult to follow? If so, spend extra time in the outlining stages; this is likely to produce a better organized final product. Do you notice your drafts are frequently subjected to numerous technical corrections? If so, focus on finishing projects even earlier, allowing more time for final polishing and detail work.

External deadlines and cost constraints limit what you can do on each project, but they should not limit what you learn about your writing and how to improve it. Reflection is key.

Failure is an opportunity.
If you blame someone else,
there is no end to the blame.

Therefore the Master
fulfills her own obligations
and corrects her own mistakes.
She does what she needs to do
and demands nothing of others. – ch. 79

CHAPTER 7: LET GO

If you want to accord with the Tao,
just do your job, then let go. – ch. 24

The law is powerful, and lawyers and others involved in the legal system play incredibly important societal roles. Yet lawyers as a group have been described as "in remarkably poor health and quite unhappy."[1] The professional demands seem, at least at times, to never end.

So the final point of this book is this: You are only human. Your job is very likely important. But once your job is done, don't worry about it. Learn from it, but don't let it consume you. Live your life, do what else is important, and try again tomorrow. There are only so many hours in the day; take your job and work seriously, but don't take yourself too seriously. As the *Tao* puts it:

> *In work, do what you enjoy.*
> *In family life, be completely present. – ch. 8*

It is often difficult to not become consumed with work. After all, we want to be successful; people trust us to help them, and the task is an important one. But our work rarely defines us. Even if it did, "success" is often shallow. The spectacular win today is likely to be balanced by a loss tomorrow. Dwelling on that terrible outcome won't change it, nor is it likely to help us get ready for a new battle. Five years from now, what work projects will you remember?

> *Success is as dangerous as failure....*
> *Whether you go up the ladder or down it,*
> *your position is shaky.*
> *When you stand with your two feet on the ground,*
> *you will always keep your balance. – ch. 13*

Furthermore, we don't always even know what is "good" and what is "bad." Sometimes an outcome that feels like a loss is, in actuality, a win; we often lack complete perspective. Consider the following story from the Huai Nan Tzu:

> A poor farmer's horse ran off into the country of the barbar-
> ians. All his neighbors offered their condolences, but his fa-

---

1. Patrick J. Schiltz, "On Being a Happy, Healthy, and Ethical Member of an Unhappy, Unhealthy, and Unethical Profession," 52 *Vand. L. Rev.* 871, 873 (1999).

ther said, "How do you know this isn't good fortune?" After a few months the horse returned with a barbarian horse of excellent stock. All his neighbors offered their congratulations, but his father said, "How do you know that this isn't a disaster?" The two horses bred, and the family became rich in fine horses. The farmer's son spent much of his time riding them; one day he fell off and broke his hipbone. All his neighbors offered the farmer their condolences, but his father said, "How do you know that this isn't good fortune?" Another year passed, and the barbarians invaded the frontier. All the able-bodied young men were conscripted, and nine-tenths of them died in the war. Thus good fortune can be disaster and vice versa. Who can tell how events will be transformed?[2]

As I was once told, life is easier when we recognize that 50% of everything that happens is because of what we do and the other 50% is because of luck. There is no point in being too dejected when we lose, nor in being too boastful when we prevail. It isn't all about us. And as pointed out in Chapter 1, even if we wanted to, we can't control everything around us:

> *Trying to control the future*
> *is like trying to take the master carpenter's place.*
> *When you handle the master carpenter's tools,*
> *chances are that you'll cut yourself. – ch. 74*

We can *influence* outcomes, but we can't *determine* them.

Work hard to improve your writing. Learn the way, be flexible, don't rush, break it down, know when to stop, and reflect. And then, let go.

> **If you realize that all things change,**
> **there is nothing you will try to hold on to. – ch. 74**

---

2. Stephen Mitchell, *Tao Te Ching: A New English Version* 112 (Perennial Classics 2000).

INDEX